BASEBALL SHORTS

1,000 OF THE GAME'S FUNNIEST ONE-LINERS

GLENN LIEBMAN

CB

CONTEMPORARY
BOOKS

CHICAGO

Library of Congress Cataloging-in-Publication Data

Liebman, Glenn.
    Baseball shorts : 1,000 of the game's funniest
one-liners / Glenn Liebman.
        p.   cm.
    ISBN 0-8092-3644-3
    1. Baseball—United States—Quotations, maxims,
etc.   2. Baseball players—United States—
Quotations.   I. Title.
GV867.3.L54   1994
796.357'0973—dc20   94-198
                                                          CIP

Published by Contemporary Books, Inc.
Two Prudential Plaza, Chicago, Illinois 60601-6790
Manufactured in the United States of America
International Standard Book Number: 0-8092-3644-3
10   9   8   7   6   5   4   3   2   1

To the two greatest people I've ever known—
my late mother, Frieda,
who taught me about courage and generosity,
and my wife, Kathy,
who personifies those virtues every day.

ACKNOWLEDGMENTS

After my last book, *Sports Shorts*, was published, I was kidded unmercifully for thanking so many people (except for my good friends Connie and Nancy). I did this based on a very logical theory: the more people you thank, the more people are forced to buy the book. With this in mind, I would like to thank everyone in the United States for making this book possible.

But seriously, there are a lot of people who helped me throughout this project, beginning with the many hilarious baseball players, writers, managers, and announcers. Thanks to my agent, Philip Spitzer, for his continued great work. This book would not have been possible without the wonderful people at Contemporary Books, including my terrific editor, Nancy Crossman, marketing director Christine Albritton, and publicist Maureen Musker. A special thanks to the nation's top sports interviewer, Roy Firestone, who took the time to interview me on "Up Close." It was an experience I will never forget.

I'd like to thank my friends and co-workers at the Alliance for the Mentally Ill of New York State—Kyla (one of the nation's most talented poets), Mame, Adeline, Ed, Steve, Rita, Harvey, Muriel Shepherd (one of the most extraordinary people I've ever met), John Nerney (a wonderful person who with his wife, Dorothy, forms the best comedy team since Laurel and Hardy, which is not surprising since I think John went to school with Stan Laurel), and Carol Saginaw (one of the most unassuming, smart, and compassionate people I have ever met who hates schmaltz as much as I love it).

I would like to thank a few close friends for their encouragement—Stu Waller (all right, so we've both lost a little hair), Jim Nolan (Mr. Real Estate), Steve Keane (the man *owns* Saratoga), David Wollner (who has made friendship and caring into an art form), Scott Sommer (all contributions to WMHT are accepted), Lou Roper (president of the Leo "Bananas" Foster and Uncle Jock Fan Club) and David Agler (I still can't believe you ate those turkey giblets).

My wonderful mother- and father-in-law, Bill and Helen Coll, and Granny Murray deserve special thanks for being my top book promoters. Thanks also to my brothers- and sisters-in-law and my niece Aimee. Thanks to my dad, Bernard, for his continued love and encouragement, my sister-in-law Deb, my gorgeous niece Samantha Anne, my brother, Bennett, easily the greatest brother in history and the president of the George Chuvalo Fan Club, my late mother, Frieda, who taught me about the importance of friendship, generosity, kindness, and love of chocolate cake. And finally I'd like to thank the most talented, courageous, and loving person I'll ever know—my wife, Kathy.

INTRODUCTION

Baseball is what drives millions of us to turn directly
to the sports section and study box scores as though
we were about to get a pop quiz on the subject (How
many hits did Olerud get yesterday? How many did
Randy Johnson strike out?), to dream up absurd hot-
stove-league trades that would help our team (Maybe
the Mets can trade Chico Walker to the White Sox for
Frank Thomas), and to follow our favorites with an
almost religious fervor.

Despite occasional carping by its critics, baseball
has captured the hearts and minds of Americans as no
other sport has ever done. The President doesn't in-
augurate the football season by throwing out an open-
ing-day football; hundreds of thousands of fans don't
flock to preseason hockey games; nor do 20,000 people travel to the induction ceremonies of the Basketball Hall of Fame.

What baseball also has done is provide us with

humor—and lots of it. This book was designed for one purpose only—to make you laugh. The one-liners of baseball's greats—Yogi, Casey, Tommy Lasorda, Rocky Bridges, Satchel Paige, Phil Rizzuto, Mickey Mantle—as well as the humor hall of famers of today—Andy Van Slyke, Charlie Hough, John Kruk, Lenny Dykstra—are all here.

Whether you are looking for a classic Jerry Coleman malaprop ("Next up is Fernando Gonzales, who is not playing tonight"), an unanswerable Larry Andersen question ("If a guy is good fastball hitter, does that mean I should throw him a bad fastball?"), a great Jim Murray insult ("Some people have a chip on their shoulder. Billy Martin has a whole lumber yard"), or just a plain hilarious line like Bo Belinsky's comment about his divorce from actress Mamie Van Doren ("I need her like Custer needs Indians")—you can find it in this book.

So take a few hours to relax and put aside conversations about long-term contracts, free agency, and television revenues and instead focus on baseball's all-time funniest one-liners.

"He doesn't have to worry about a hockey game getting rained out in the middle of the second period."

> *Joe DiMaggio, on comparisons between his legendary hitting streak and Wayne Gretzky's scoring streak in hockey*

"Hell, Lou, it took you 15 years to get out of the game. Sometimes I'm out in 15 minutes."

> *Lefty Gomez, after Lou Gehrig ended his consecutive-game streak*

"First triple I ever had."

> *Lefty Gomez, a weak-hitting pitcher, on having triple-bypass surgery*

"If Lew could cook, I'd marry him."

> *Fred Haney, Braves manager, after Lew Burdette won three games for the Braves in the 1957 World Series*

"I'm going to have to get a little hot. Has anyone ever won 40 back to back?"

> Charlie Hough, asked after winning his 200th game, at the age of 40, when he would reach the 300-win plateau

"I guess I'd better send my fingers to Cooperstown."

> Dennis Lamp, after giving up Lou Brock's 3,000th base hit

"If you act like you know what you're doing, you can do anything you want—except neurosurgery."

> John Lowenstein

"The Birch Society is going to expel Eric for making a Red famous."

> Graig Nettles, after Eric Show, a member of the John Birch Society, gave up Pete Rose's record-breaking hit

"I'm no different from anybody else with two arms, two legs, and 4,200 hits."

> Pete Rose

"No, I had 999 times to get ready for it."

> *Kent Tekulve, asked if he was nervous playing in his 1,000th game*

"Well, they did have a Bob Uecker Day Off for me once in Philly."

> *Bob Uecker, asked if they ever had a day for him as a player*

ADVERTISEMENTS/ COMMERCIALS

"Reggie Jackson wouldn't get into the batter's box until he knew we were back from commercial. Of course, Uecker wanted to hit during the commercial."

> *Al Michaels*

"The people from Jockey were with me to make sure I was wearing my underwear."

> *Jim Palmer, on his induction into the Hall of Fame*

"I want to be like Maxwell House coffee—good to the last drop."

> *Don Sutton, on how he envisioned his career ending*

ADVICE

"If a young guy asked me for advice on how to get into broadcasting, I'd say, 'Hit .350 or win the Heisman.' "
> *Skip Caray*

"I wish I could remember everything I told him."
> *Charlie Hough, after Bobby Witt asked him for advice and then proceeded to win eight games in a row*

AGE

"I refuse to call a 47-year-old white-haired man Sparky."
> *Al Clark, umpire, on Sparky Anderson*

"There are younger Aztec ruins."
Bill Conlin, on Vicente Romo

"Tommy John is so old, he uses Absorbine Senior."
Bob Costas

"The Houston Astros are the youngest team in the National League if you judge by age."
Don Drysdale

"I'm throwing twice as hard, but the ball is getting there half as fast."
Yankees Hall of Famer Lefty Gomez

"Say Satch, tell me, was Abraham Lincoln a crouch hitter?"
Lefty Gomez, poking fun at the ageless Satchel Paige

"When I broke in, they didn't have bats—we just grabbed the branch off a tree."
Charlie Hough

"My wife doesn't like it. She says everyone thinks she's also 44."

> *Tommy John, on the press constantly referring to his age*

"If you don't have a bad back by the time you're 60, then you haven't done anything in your life."

> *Joe Morgan, former Red Sox manager*

"The average age of our bench is deceased."

> *Tommy Lasorda, on the Dodgers bench of Vic Davalillo and Manny Mota*

"Pudge is so old, they didn't have a history class when he went to school."

> *Steve Lyons, on Carlton Fisk*

"Girls used to come up to me and say, 'My sister loves you.' Now they say, 'My mother loves you.' "

> *Lee Mazzilli*

"When you're 21, you're a prospect; when you're 30, you're a suspect."

> *Jim McGlothlin, as a pitcher with the White Sox*

"When I was younger, yes."

> *Danny Murtaugh, asked on his 57th birthday if he could have a better wish than the Pirates winning the World Series*

"I don't know how old I am because the goat ate the Bible that had my birth certificate in it. The goat lived to be 27."

> *Satchel Paige*

"I don't play like a 40-year-old, and I don't think like a 40-year-old. I guess that's because I'm 41."

> *Pete Rose*

"Doctors tell me I have the body of a 30-year-old. I know I have the brain of a 15-year-old. If you got both, you can play baseball."

> *Pete Rose*

"The trick is growing up without growing old."

> *Casey Stengel*

"I used to pitch, golf, have fun, rest, and pitch again. Now I pitch, recover, recover, recover, rest, and pitch again."

Don Sutton

AGENTS

"When they smile, blood drips off their teeth."
Ted Turner

AIRPLANES

"There wasn't too much of a delay. We only had to change a spark plug and 30 pairs of shorts."

Don Drysdale, on the emergency landing of the Dodgers' private jet

"We've got a problem here. Luis Tiant wants to use the bathroom, and it says no foreign objects on the toilet."

Graig Nettles, on an airplane flight with his Cuban teammate

"Jack Daniels stock doesn't drop when I'm flying between baseball games."

Rusty Staub, on his fear of flying

"I don't know how close we came, but the lady in 13D in the other plane was having the chicken dinner."

Jim Sundberg, on his plane nearly colliding with another plane

ALL-STAR GAME

"I don't really go to compete. I go to be seen."

Reggie Jackson, on his many All-Star Game appearances

"To me it felt like 70 degrees with a nice breeze."

Mike Piazza, on playing in his first All-Star Game in 95-degree heat in Baltimore

"If I ain't startin', I ain't departin'."

Garry Templeton, on refusing to attend the 1979 All-Star Game because he wasn't chosen to start

ARBITRATION

"It's great when it's all over and the arbiter asks, 'What's a save?' "

Whitey Herzog

"I knew I was in trouble when the arbiter asked what we meant by such symbols as IP, BB, and ERA."

Greg Minton

ARTIFICIAL TURF

"If a horse can't eat it, then I don't like it."

Dick Allen

ASSISTS

"It doesn't matter if his shoulder's sore. He doesn't throw anyone out anyway."

> *Sparky Anderson, on Kirk Gibson having one assist in 298 chances during the 1985 season*

"Brenly said he threw the glove around the infield."

> *Mike Krukow, on Terry Mulholland flipping his glove with the ball in it to first baseman Bob Brenly*

ASTRODOME

"This is a tough yard for the hitter when the air conditioner is blowing in."

> *Bob Boone*

ATTENDANCE

"Both have been real nice."

> *Bob Brenly, on the fans' acceptance of the Giants despite a bad season*

"It was so quiet, I heard a guy in the upper deck burp, and then I heard a woman in the left field stands yell, 'Pardon you.'"

> *Bill Caudill, on the small crowd at the Metrodome*

"That's not a crowd; that's my shirt size."

> *Hank Greenwald, on the attendance figure of 1,632 at a Giants game*

"Open a service station in center field."

> *Dave Heaverlo, on how to increase attendance in Oakland during a gas shortage*

"It looks like a graveyard with lights."

> *Whitey Herzog, on a small crowd at Candlestick Park*

"It was the first time in history that everyone in the stands got a foul ball."

> *Dave LaPoint, on one day at Candlestick Park*

"Some people have those games where you guess the number of people in the park. Here you have to identify them too."

> *Lee Mazzilli, on the attendance at Three Rivers Stadium*

"It was like playing a midnight game in the loser's bracket of one of those softball tournaments."

> *Bill Wegman, on playing before a quiet, small crowd at Anaheim Stadium*

AUTOGRAPHS

"I didn't know whether to call the pitch or get his autograph."

> *Joe Garagiola, on playing against Ted Williams for the first time in the 1946 World Series*

"My autograph may not be worth much now, but five years from now it will be worth even less."

Tommy Lasorda

"Every time I sign a ball, and there have been thousands, I thank my luck that I wasn't born Coveleski or Wambsganss or Peckinpaugh."

Mel Ott

"It was fun until a kid came up to me and said, 'My dad says you're getting old, you're going to die, and your autographs will be valuable.' "

Warren Spahn, on an autograph show

"I love signing autographs. I'll sign anything but veal cutlets. My ballpoint pen slips on veal cutlets."

Casey Stengel

AWARDS

"MVP on the worst team ever. Just how do they mean that?"

Richie Ashburn, MVP of the 1962 Mets

"I knew I'd never win the Cy Young Award, so I was trying to be Fireman of the Year."

> *Bert Blyleven, on helping to extinguish a fire*

"I just won the Nobel Prize of baseball."

> *Elston Howard, 1963 American League MVP*

"If I was ever going to get an award, I never thought it would be in Boston."

> *Don Zimmer, on winning an award from sportswriters for his long baseball career in Boston*

BABIES

"All I wanted was a healthy baby that could switch-hit."

> *Jim Lefebvre, on his new baby*

"He was so big, he walked out of the delivery room by himself."

> *Dave Smith, on the birth of his nine-pound, six-ounce son*

BAD DAYS

"He got hit so hard, I had to get all the married men off the field."

> *Whitey Herzog, on Ken Dayley*

"I know, Jim, but the outfielders are."

> *Jeff Torborg, after Jim Kern was taken out of a game but insisted he wasn't tired*

BAD LUCK

"He had Whitey Ford's stuff and Edsel Ford's luck."

> *Richie Ashburn, on former Mets pitcher Ken MacKenzie*

"One of two things is happening. Either Miller has come back and is out there somewhere or we've been very bad."

Sparky Anderson, on the Tigers' losing eight straight games so Anderson was unable to pass Miller Huggins on the all-time managerial wins list

"We're not so bad as people thought, although that's not saying much."

Buddy Bell, on the Texas Rangers

"Throw a tent over us—we're a three-ring circus."

Johnny Bench, on a bad Reds team

"Have you ever seen a mechanic work on a car without tools?"

Vida Blue, on being backed up by a lousy Oakland A's team

"For the Washington Senators, the worst time of year is the baseball season."

Roger Kahn

"If they keep this team together, we could finish 30 out."

Dave LaPoint, on a bad Giants team

"In Los Angeles, finding a celebrity to throw out the first ball is not a problem. The hard part is finding a Dodger who can catch it."

Jay Leno

"It makes you rethink the importance of being in the major leagues."

Jim Marshall, on managing the last-place Oakland A's

"With the Padres, you'd get off to a four-and-one start, and that would be the highlight of the year."

Steve Mura

"Our phenoms aren't phenomenating."

Lefty Phillips, explaining why the Angels were having a bad year

"I'm 49 years old, and I'd like to live to be 50."

Eddie Sawyer, on why he quit managing a bad Phillies team

"I'm not interested in selling the Braves . . . but I don't know why."

Ted Turner

"Last year we had so many people coming in and out, they didn't bother to sew the name on the back of the uniform. They put their names on with Velcro."

Andy Van Slyke, on a bad Pirates team

"You can't ask Mr. Ed to keep up with Secretariat."

Andy Van Slyke, on the Pirates trying to catch up to the rest of their division

BARS

"I decided to get out when my bartender was driving a Caddy and I was driving a Chevy."

Billy Gardner, on why he gave up owning a bar

"They've never been on a baseball field. Anybody can play ball in a saloon."

Fred Hutchinson, on second-guessers

"When Billy Martin reaches for a bar tab, his arm shrinks six inches."

Tommy Lasorda

"I never had any serious conversations with Owens because I never went into bars."

Lonnie Smith, on his former manager Paul Owens

BASEBALL CARDS

"They've taken my playing record off and put my managerial record on."

Sparky Anderson, on why he likes his latest baseball cards

"I was amazed when some kids [at a grade school] asked if I ever pitched to Mickey Mantle or Harmon Killebrew. I thought, 'There's some good in baseball cards after all.' But then I got upset when a few of them asked if I ever pitched to Babe Ruth or Honus Wagner."

Moe Drabowsky

"I've asked the bubblegum people to change the back of my card to read, 'In Military Service' or 'Out to Lunch.' "

> *Charlie Kerfeld, after a lousy 1987 season*

"My mother must have sent my baby picture; that was the last time I weighed 175."

> *Charlie Kerfeld, on being listed on his baseball card as 5'11", 175 pounds when he was 6'6", 245 pounds*

"All I know is it used to take 43 Marv Throneberry cards to get one Carl Furillo."

> *Marv Throneberry*

BASEBALL WISDOM

"In the seventh inning, the fans get up and sing 'Take Me Out to the Ball Game,' and you're already there. It's really a stupid thing to say."

> *Larry Andersen*

"You spend a good piece of your life gripping a baseball, and it turns out it was the other way around all the time."

Jim Bouton

"I'm not sure what it means, but when the ball is not in play, somebody grabs his crotch."

Paula Bouton

"Baseball is not a game of inches like you hear people say. It's a game of hundredths of inches."

Rube Bressler

"The first big-league game I ever saw was at the Polo Grounds. My father took me. I remember it so well—the green grass and green stands. It was like seeing Oz."

John Curtis

"Baseball players are the weirdest of all. I think it's all that organ music."

Peter Gent

"Knowin' all about baseball is just about as profitable as bein' a good whittler."

Kin Hubbard

"Whatever is going to happen is going to happen when it happens, regardless of what happens."
Mike LaValliere

"Baseball is simple. All you have to do is sit on your butt, spit tobacco, and nod at the stupid things your manager says."
Bill Lee

"Baseball is the blessed silence that comes between Dick Vitale and John Madden."
Bernie Lincicome, sportswriter

"Baseball's got it all wrong—the stars get the dough, and the other actors get scale."
Walter Matthau

"I don't think any of us have really grown up, because we've been doing the same thing since we were eight years old."
Dale Murphy

"There is no homework."
Dan Quisenberry, on the best thing about baseball

"I'm glad I don't play anymore. I could never learn all those handshakes."

Phil Rizzuto

"Ninety feet between bases is perhaps as close as man has ever come to perfection."

Red Smith

"Baseball is dull only to those with dull minds."

Red Smith

"Ability is the act of getting credit for all the home runs someone else hits."

Casey Stengel

"The best thing about baseball is that you can do something about yesterday tomorrow."

Manny Trillo

"Every season has its peaks and valleys. What you have to try to eliminate is the Grand Canyon."

Andy Van Slyke

"Good pitching always stops good hitting and vice versa."

Bob Veale

"Baseball is the only game left for people. To play basketball now, you have to be 7′6″. To play football, you have to be the same width."

Bill Veeck

"The most beautiful thing in the world is a ballpark filled with people."

Bill Veeck

"There ain't much to being a ballplayer if you're a ballplayer."

Honus Wagner

"You can't sit on a lead and run a few plays into the line and just kill the clock. You've got to throw the ball over the goddamn plate and give the other team a chance."

Earl Weaver

"Hitters get to scratch themselves only once per at-bat."

> Tom Weir, sportswriter, on how to speed up the game

"Baseball is like church. Many attend, but few understand."

> Wes Westrum

"Baseball is the only field of endeavor in which a man can succeed three times out of ten and be considered a good performer."

> Ted Williams

BATTING STANCES

"Because you don't get to hit in the bullpen."

> Bob Uecker, on not alternating his batting stance

BED CHECKS

"The manager used to have a bed check for me every night. No problem; my bed was always there."
Bob Veale

BEER

"Beer makes some people happy. Cashing checks makes me delirious with joy."
Jim Brosnan

"I still get to sleep at night. It just takes a few more beers."

Jackie Moore, on rumors of his being fired

"Baseball is the working man's game. A baseball crowd is a beer-drinking crowd, not a mixed-drink crowd."

Bill Veeck

BENCH

"I'm being showcased on the bench. They have me sitting where people can see me."
Ron Gardenhire

"I have so many splinters from sitting on the bench that if somebody struck a match, I might catch fire."
Billy Grabarkewitz

"I told you we'd improve our bench."
Jack McKeon, on renovation of the San Diego dugout

BLEACHERS

"They were so high, I could high-five with the guys in the blimp."
Tommy Lasorda, on the lousy seats he used to get

"The sun is hotter, and the beer is cooler."
Bill Veeck, on the bleachers

BODIES

"He has an upper body like Charles Atlas and a lower body like Lana Turner."
Whitey Herzog, on Pedro Guerrero

"Just to have his body, I'd trade mine and my wife's and throw in some cash."
Pete Rose, on Mike Schmidt

BOOKS

"I'm supposed to be writing a book, and I can hardly read."
Mark Fidrych

"If I ever decide to do a book, I've already got the title—*The Bases Were Loaded and So Was I.*"

Jim Fregosi

"It would be called *I Hate the Game But I Love Drinking the Beer.*"

Kent Hrbek, on his autobiography

"One of them has me dead already."

Mark Koenig, on why he doesn't trust any books written about the 1927 Yankees

"I passed my time reading a book. It was called *J.F.K.—The Man and the Airport.*"

Joe Magrane, on recuperating from an injury

"You have to give Pete credit for what he accomplished. He went to college, and the only book he ever read was *The Pete Rose Story.*"

Karolyn Rose, Pete Rose's ex-wife

"I guess I could have written two books of my life— one for the adults and one for the kids."

Babe Ruth

BOOS

"It's the first time in my career I was booed coming into a game. Usually they boo after I leave."
Bob Stanley

BOREDOM

"Having to listen to someone talk about themselves when I want to talk about me."
Tom Paciorek, defining boredom

BUSINESS

"The reason baseball calls itself a game, I believe, is that it is too screwed up to be a business."
Jim Bouton

"Everybody thinks of baseball as a sacred cow. When you have the nerve to challenge it, people look down their noses at you. There are a lot of things wrong with a lot of industries . . . baseball is one of them."

> *Curt Flood, Cardinals outfielder whose legal challenge to baseball's reserve clause system paved the way for free agency*

"It's a business. If I could make more money down in the zinc mines, I'd be mining zinc."

> *Roger Maris*

CANADA

"We forgot about the Canadian exchange rate, so it's really only 82 mph."

> *Mike Flanagan, on Mike Boddicker's fastball being clocked at 88 mph against Toronto*

"Sure, I'm proud to be an American."

> *Steve Foster, of the Reds, when asked by a Canadian customs agent if he had anything to declare*

"There ought to be a clause in our contract allowing us to veto a country."

>*Steve Renko, on being traded to the Expos*

CANDLESTICK PARK

"Candlestick Park is the ninth blunder of the world."

>*Herb Caen, writer*

"It's like playing a game on an aircraft carrier in the North Atlantic."

>*Rich Donnelly, Pirates third-base coach*

"The coldest winter I ever spent was a summer in San Francisco."

>*Charlie Dressen*

"Candlestick was built on the water. It should have been built under it."

>*Roger Maris*

"This wouldn't be such a bad place to play if it wasn't for the wind. I guess that's like saying hell wouldn't be such a bad place if it wasn't for the heat."
Jerry Reuss

"The only difference between Candlestick and San Quentin is that at Candlestick they let you go home at night."
Jim Wohlford

CARDINALS

"Tradition here in St. Louis is Stan Musial coming to the clubhouse and making the rounds. Tradition in San Diego is Nate Colbert coming into the clubhouse and trying to sell you a used car."
Bob Shirley

CAREER

"You slow up a half step and it's the beginning of your last ball game. It might take a few years, but you're on your way out."

Pete Reiser

"I'd better make it, because I can't sing or dance and they've already got a pitching coach."

Don Sutton, on trying to make the Dodgers at the end of his career

CHAMPAGNE

"The champagne they're keeping in the locker room is getting more valuable every year."

Johnny Carson, on the one advantage of the Angels always losing in the end

"Why champagne? It doesn't taste good, and it stings the eyes. Why not milk? Or even half-and-half?"

Rich Donnelly, on clubhouse celebrations

CHARACTERS

"The most amazing thing I've ever seen was Jay Johnstone in uniform in line at a concession stand at Dodger Stadium after a game had already started."
        Fred Claire, Dodgers GM

"In all the years I played, he was the only guy who ever scared me, and he was on my team."
        Ron Fairly, on Stan Williams

"If he turned pro, he'd put us all out of business."
        George Gobel, on the wit of Casey Stengel

"Now that Jose's in Texas, I'll be expecting him to hit 60 home runs and drive 55."
        Ann Richards, governor of Texas, on Jose Canseco

"If everyone were like him, I wouldn't play. I'd find a safer way to make a living."
        Andy Van Slyke, on Mitch "Wild Thing" Williams

CLOTHES

"My wife bought me a tie for $135. For $135, it should tie itself."

Wally Backman

"He's the only guy I know who does his clothes shopping at the San Diego Zoo. He puts five animals on the endangered species list with one outfit."

Bob Brenly, on Kevin Mitchell

"I've found that you don't need to wear a necktie if you can hit."

Ted Williams

CLUBHOUSE MEETINGS

"The only clubhouse meetings I like are the ones dividing up playoff shares."

Billy Gardner

"I've had managers who had 30-minute meetings but quit making sense after 30 seconds."
Richie Hebner

COACHING

"The best qualification a coach can have is being the manager's drinking buddy."
Jim Bouton

"The main quality a great third-base coach must have is a fast runner."
Rocky Bridges

"All coaches religiously carry fungo bats in the spring to ward off suggestions that they are not working."
Jim Brosnan

"Throw strikes. Don't worry about home runs. Babe Ruth is dead."
Art Fowler, on standard advice he gives as a pitching coach

"Hitters have maids. Baseball teams have coaches."

Jose Martinez, former Royals coach

"Just act like you're listening to me. I'll leave in a couple of minutes. Promise."

Leo Mazzone, Atlanta Braves pitching coach, explaining what he says to left-hander Steve Avery when he visits the mound to give relief pitchers more time to warm up

"When I'm feeling good, I'm a player; when I'm feeling bad, I'm a coach."

Lou Piniella, on being a player/coach with the Yankees

"The game sure has changed since I played."

John Wathan, a few minutes after retiring as a player and becoming a coach

"How could it be mental? I don't have a college education."

>*Steve Farr, asked whether his shoulder soreness was a mental problem*

"I wound up with more complete games than credits."

>*Mike Flanagan, on his pitching days at the University of Massachusetts*

"I majored in eligibility."

>*Tim Laudner*

"He was like a college professor. I thought he had tenure."

>*Mike Macfarlane, on Bobby Valentine being fired after eight years as the Rangers manager*

COLLISIONS

"They're going to have to hang a bell around one of their necks."

> *Larry Haney, after teammates Brian Downing and Gary Pettis collided twice in four days*

"I felt like I collided with a Mercedes Benzinger."

> *Dennis Lamp, on bumping into teammate Todd Benzinger*

COMEBACKS

"I was thinking about making a comeback until I pulled a muscle vacuuming."

> *Johnny Bench, after Carlton Fisk passed him on the all-time home run list for catchers*

"This winter I'm working out every day, throwing at a wall. I'm 11–0 against the wall."

Jim Bouton

"This man deserves the Comeback Player of the Year for this game alone."

Roger Craig, on Bob Brenly commit-ting four errors in a game and then hitting a game-winning home run

"There must be some mistake. I've never been away."

Dick Donovan, on finishing second in the voting for Comeback Player of the Year Award

"I'm pleased, but I would have preferred not being in the position of being eligible for such an award."

Willie McCovey, on winning the Comeback Player of the Year Award

"All I know is that I've won every award there is to win in this game except Comeback Player of the Year—which I'll get next year."

Pete Rose after a bad year

"Bowie Kuhn is the best commissioner in baseball today."

> *Jim Bouton, during Kuhn's tenure as commissioner*

"I have often called Bowie Kuhn the village idiot. I apologize to all the village idiots of America. He's the nation's idiot."

> *Charles Finley*

"Move the mound in, raise it, dim the lights, and play all night games."

> *Charlie Hough, asked what he would do if he were baseball commissioner*

"He can stay retired and still be commissioner. That's what they want anyway."

> *John Lowenstein, on Lee MacPhail saying he'd rather be retired than be commissioner*

"If I could be commissioner for a day, I'd play one game a year versus sportswriters to illustrate how easy the game is."

Joe Magrane

"I'm not very smart. I think I can prove that. Who would accept a job with Marge Schott's dog, Ted Turner, and George Steinbrenner as your boss?"

Peter Ueberroth

COMPLETE GAMES

"Your pitchers have more complete games this year than you do."

Whitey Herzog, on Hal McRae being thrown out of several games during the 1993 season

"There should be a commonsense clause in his contract."

> *Jim Frey, on Steve Trout falling off a bike and missing a start*

"Your life or mine?"

> *Whitey Herzog, on being offered a lifetime contract by 80-year-old Cardinal's owner Gussie Busch*

"Thanks a million."

> *Tommy Lasorda, after getting a new contract from Dodger's owner Peter O'Malley*

"He told me he thinks this is the last contract I have to do for him. He told me that six times before."

> *Dick Moss, Nolan Ryan's agent*

"It's gonna be fun buying a condo every two weeks."

> *Don Slaught, after signing a three-year contract for $3 million*

"If you lose five in a row in New York, the general manager gets fired. Here he gets a lifetime contract."

John Wathan, after John Schuerholz, former Royals GM, signed a 15-year contract

CONTROL

"I had a lot of no-hitters in the minors. They were games when I didn't hit anybody."

Jim Kern

"He could have knocked a gnat off a hitter's nose."

Bob Skinner, on Harvey Haddix

"I was so wild, I could have walked Manute Bol four times."

Walt Terrell

COURTESY

"You wanna be a bat boy? Don't ever do that again."
> *Dick Williams, after his catcher gave the opposing hitter the bat after a foul ball*

COWS

"I didn't try too hard. I was afraid I'd get emotionally involved with the cow."
> *Rocky Bridges, on being second in a milking contest*

CRIME AND PUNISHMENT

"They must have been an expansion gang."
> *Gene Mauch, on one gang's having faulty ammunition during a gang war*

"The way he fielded ground balls, I knew he was going to wind up on the bench."

Sam Mele, on former college team-mate Judge Burton Roberts

"The last time I smiled so much was for a jury."

Pascual Perez, on winning his fourth game in a row

CUBS

"Good things come to those who wait . . . and wait . . . and wait."

Ernie Banks, on the Cubs winning the division in 1984

"I don't know why we bought the Cubs. We already had a perfectly good company softball team."

Bob Verdi, after the (Chicago) Tribune Company purchased the Cubs in 1981

CUBS FANS

"One thing you can learn as a Cubs fan: when you buy your tickets, you can bank on seeing the bottom of the ninth."

Joe Garagiola

CURSING

"I have an off-season vocabulary and a during-season vocabulary."

Elliott Maddox

CURVEBALLS

"Tom Lasorda's curveball had as much hang time as a Ray Guy punt."

Rocky Bridges

"Do you realize that even as we sit here, we are hurtling through space at a tremendous rate of speed? Think about it. Our world is just a hanging curveball."
Bill Lee

"He calls for the curveball so much. He can't hit it, so he figures nobody else can."
Casey Stengel, on Chris Cannizzaro

DEATH

"When I was in the hospital, I heard my wife say she was going to cremate me. I decided to get better because I couldn't take the heat."
Ellis Clary

"If Casey Stengel were alive today, he'd be spinning in his grave."
Ralph Kiner

"He can pitch when he's relaxed, and he'll be happy and relaxed here. If he isn't, we'll kill him."
John Kruk, on the Phillies acquiring Mark Davis

"I bleed Dodger blue, and when I die, I'm going to the Big Dodger in the sky."

> *Tommy Lasorda*

"Well, that kind of puts a damper even on a Yankee win."

> *Phil Rizzuto, on the news that the pope had died, 1978*

DEFENSE

"How do you spell Offerman? An *o*, two *f*s and 50 *e*s."

> *Anonymous, on Dodger's shortstop Jose Offerman's fielding*

"They should have called a welder."

> *Richie Ashburn, on Dave Kingman's glove being repaired*

"If you don't catch the ball, you catch the bus home."

> *Yogi Berra*

"It's like asking Patrick Ewing to play point guard."

Hubie Brooks, on moving from short-stop to right field

"I've seen better hands on a clock."

Mel Durslag, sportswriter, after Bill Russell made five errors in a double-header

"They want me to play third like Brooks Robinson, but I think I play it more like Mel Brooks."

Tim Flannery

"A great catch is like watching girls go by—the last one you see is always the prettiest."

Bob Gibson, after a great catch by Curt Flood

"That's like comparing a crack in a sidewalk to the San Andreas fault."

Tom Glavine, comparing the Braves' defense of 1993 to that of the late '80s

"I never knew what Joe DiMaggio looked like until I roomed with him. All I ever saw was the back of his uniform after I threw a pitch."

Lefty Gomez

"You know you're in trouble when you say 'Nice catch' and it's the catcher you're talking about."

Hank Greenwald, after catcher Mark Salas had four passed balls in a game

"First I pray to God that nobody hits the ball to me. Then I pray to God nobody hits the ball to Steve Sax."

Pedro Guerrero

"Catching the ball is a pleasure. Knowing what to do with it is a business."

Tommy Henrich

"The best part is, all I have to do is catch balls instead of throwing them. I didn't care for throwing that much."

Gregg Jefferies, on moving from second base to first

"They're going to name a glove after you."

Lynn Jones, after some good fielding plays by Glenn Wilson

"If you hit [Luis] Polonia 100 fly balls, you could make a movie out of it—*Catch-22*."

Dennis Lamp

"In the outfield, fly balls are my only weakness."

Carmelo Martinez

"You just stand behind him [Hack Wilson] and you'll get more baseballs than you know what to do with."

Joe McCarthy, when a boy asked him for a ball

"They've got to hit him a million ground balls. I've hit him my million."

Ed Nottles, Pawtucket manager, advising the Red Sox on how to improve Sam Horn's fielding

"Our fielders have to catch a lot of balls—or at least deflect them to someone who can."

Dan Quisenberry, on the Royals' fielding

"I can still steal bases. I can still run. I can still hit. I can still make errors."
Lonnie Smith

"Bobby Brown reminds me of a fellow who's been hitting for 12 years and fielding one."
Casey Stengel

"We got a guy on our club who has such bad hands, his glove is embarrassed."
Frank Sullivan

"They had better defense at Pearl Harbor."
Andy Van Slyke, on the Pirates

DESIGNATED HITTERS

"I wish I was still in baseball. The designated hitter rule was made for me."
Dean Chance, on a lifetime batting average of .066

"I flush the toilets between innings to keep my wrists strong."

John Lowenstein, on being a DH

"I'll go into the clubhouse between innings and eat hot dogs."

Fred Lynn

"In high schools, colleges, and some countries, they're learning a game that's not baseball."

Tug McGraw, on the DH

"The designated hitter rule is like letting someone else take Wilt Chamberlain's free throws."

Rick Wise

DINNER

"You feel like a starting pitcher. Afterwards you need three days' rest."

Joe Garagiola, on going to dinner with Tommy Lasorda

"You'd invite this team over for dinner, but you'd cover your furniture with plastic before we arrive."
John Kruk, on the 1993 Phillies

DIVORCE

"I need her like Custer needs Indians."
Bo Belinsky, on his breakup with actress wife Mamie Van Doren

"Nobody can be a success in two national pastimes."
Jimmy Cannon, sportswriter, on the divorce of Joe DiMaggio and Marilyn Monroe

"I never realized how short a month is until I started paying alimony."
Harry Caray

"I think my ex-wife has a voodoo doll working against me."
Bob Ojeda

"I only gave up three runs—Rosie gets half of everything."

> *Jose Rijo, on giving up six runs in an exhibition game while in the middle of a divorce*

DODGERS FANS

"People in southern California would leave early from sex."

> *Scott Ostler, sportswriter*

DOUBLEHEADERS

"I never knew anybody who said they liked doubleheaders except Ernie Banks, and I think he was lying."
> *Mike Hargrove*

"The only thing worse than a Mets game is a Mets doubleheader."
> *Casey Stengel*

"Gin was his tonic."

Al Drooz, sportswriter, on Hack Wilson

"A revival of the two Martinez lunch."

Richard Griffin, Expos PR director, on Dennis Martinez and Ramon Martinez pitching against each other

"It depends on the length of the game."

King Kelly, asked if he drank during the game

"I drink after wins. I drink after losses. I drink after rainouts."

Bob Lemon

"There is much less drinking now than there was before 1927, because I quit drinking on May 24th, 1927."

Rabbit Maranville

"No, the fast highball."

Gene Mauch, on being asked if Dick Allen's weakness was a high fastball

"Ten-thirty! I'm not even done throwing up at that hour."

Jim Pagliaroni, on being hung over and having to go to practice

"They say some of my stars drink whiskey, but I have found that the ones who drink milk shakes don't win any ball games."

Casey Stengel

"He doesn't drink, he doesn't smoke, he doesn't chew, he doesn't stay out late, and he still only hits .250."

Casey Stengel, on Bobby Richardson

"I've never played drunk; hung over, yes, but never drunk."

Hack Wilson

"Closed."

Yogi Berra, asked what he liked best about school

"In high school, I took a little English, some science, and some hubcaps and some wheel covers."
Gates Brown

"I didn't do so great in the first grade either."

Dizzy Dean, on quitting school after the second grade

"I did a report on it in the sixth grade, the seventh grade, the eighth grade, and I eventually got an *A* in the ninth grade."

Pete Rose, on doing a book report on Lou Gehrig

"Yes, but with the highest earned run average."

Casey Stengel, responding to Ken MacKenzie's "Do you realize I'm the lowest-paid member of the Yale class of 1959?"

"I'm not the brightest guy in the world. If my dad hadn't been principal of my high school, I never would have graduated."

Andy Van Slyke

"Because the track coach was the biology teacher and I had trouble with biology. I'm not crazy."

Claudell Washington, on why he took track in high school

EGO

"My only regret in life is that I can't sit in the stands and watch me pitch."

Bo Belinsky

"After Jackie Robinson, the most important black in baseball history is Reggie Jackson. I really mean that."

Reggie Jackson

"I had the greatest career anyone could ever have. I rode a big black horse. I rode hard. They heard me coming three and four towns away."

Reggie Jackson

"Charles Finley is a self-made man who worships his creator."

Jim Murray

"There's only one thing bigger than me, and that's my ego."

Dave Parker

"Me."

Pete Rose, asked who he would be if he could be any player in baseball history

"My wife. So I could see how wonderful it is to live with me."

Andy Van Slyke, asked whom he'd like to change places with for a day

ELEVATORS

"All I know is he wasn't carrying a gun."

Cal Ripken, Sr., on riding 21 floors in an elevator with a guy wearing only his socks

EXPECTATIONS

"What's one home run? If you hit one, they are going to want you to hit two."

Mick Kelleher

"Never win 20 games in a year, because they'll expect you to do it every year."

Billy Loes

EXPERIENCE

"It's what you learn after you know it all that counts."

Earl Weaver

"You don't think experience means anything until you have it."

Walt Weiss

EXTRA INNINGS

"One of our guys slid into second base in the first inning, and his scab had healed by the end of the game."

Rich Bernaldo, coach of Hillsborough (Florida) Community College baseball team, on a 32-inning game

"I've had marriages that didn't last that long."

Skip Caray, on an 11-inning game between the Giants and the Braves

FAME

"You know when you got it made? When you get your name in the crossword puzzle."

Rocky Bridges

"I used to be the toast of Toronto. Now I'm the jelly."

Lloyd Moseby

"I never had a great nickname. Haven't done any drugs. What makes news? Flakes. Being a weirdo."

Mike Schmidt, on why he never achieved the fame he deserved

FASTBALLS

"If a guy is a good fastball hitter, does that mean I should throw him a bad fastball?"

Larry Andersen

"Nobody knows how fast I am. The ball doesn't get to the mitt that often."

Lefty Gomez

"Ryan is the only guy who puts fear in me. Not because he can get you out but because he can kill you."

Reggie Jackson, on Nolan Ryan

"My fastball."

Tommy John, asked if he was missing anything after a clubhouse burglary

"Teams can't prepare for me in batting practice. They can't find anyone who throws as slow as I do."
Dave LaPoint

"I knew I was in trouble when they started clocking my fastball with a sundial."
Joe Magrane

"Once a pitcher loses his fastball, he has to go to the garbage."
Jim O'Toole, former major-league baseball player who became a public relations director for a sanitation firm

FATHERS

"Playing for Yogi is like playing for your father. Playing for Billy [Martin] is like playing for your father-in-law."
Don Baylor

"Our similarities are different."

> *Dale Berra, on the inevitable comparisons between him and his father*

"My question is, do people think I got married and had three kids just so I could play? I met my wife in kindergarten. It's not like I went through the National League Green Book looking for general managers with daughters."

> *Greg Booker, on playing for his father-in-law, Jack McKeon, in San Diego*

"He's like my daddy. If he weren't white, he'd look like my daddy."

> *Oil Can Boyd, on John McNamara*

"They shouldn't throw at me. I'm the father of five or six kids."

> *Tito Fuentes*

"On Father's Day, we again wish you all happy birthday."

> *Ralph Kiner*

"When I saw the left-field fence, I thought we were going to play softball."

Joaquin Andujar

"I don't know. I've never pitched in a phone booth before."

Gene Conley

"Do they leave it there during games?"

Bill Lee, upon first seeing the Green Monster, Fenway Park's 37-foot-high left-field wall

FIGHTS

"I'll take you and a player to be named later."

Dick Radatz, on being 6'6", 265 pounds and going after the 5'5", 165-pound Fred Patek during a bench-clearing brawl

"The receptionist said, 'Good to see you again, Albert.'"

> *Albert Belle, on being disciplined frequently by the Commissioner's office*

"It's a tax write-off."

> *Bob Boone, on getting fined for being ejected*

"That's more than I expectorated."

> *Frenchy Bordagaray, on being fined $50 for spitting*

"I don't believe in meaningless fines. When I fine a guy, I get so deep in his wallet, he thinks I'm in his socks."

> *Doc Edwards*

"The cops picked me up on a street at 3:00 A.M. and fined me $500 for being drunk and $100 for being with the Phillies."

> *Bob Uecker*

FITNESS

"He told me I was in great shape—if I was 60."
Charlie Hough, 45

"I tried real hard not to get any muscles so I wouldn't hurt them."

Dan Quisenberry, on his off-season preparation

"I'm doing now about what I did in spring training when I played—about an eighth of a sit-up, which kind of wears me out."

Bob Uecker, on recovering from an operation

FOOD

"Birds eat those things. I told the team I'm afraid some of you guys might start molting on me or maybe go to the bathroom on newspaper."

Rocky Bridges, on players who eat sunflower seeds

"I prefer fast foods."

> *Rocky Bridges, on why he doesn't eat snails*

"The games go quicker, and you can get back to the clubhouse and eat."

> *Ivan Calderon, on why he prefers playing for the Expos over the White Sox*

"What are you going to eat? Redwoods?"

> *John Candelaria, on Dave Parker's plans to become a vegetarian*

"I'm a light eater. When it gets light, I start eating."

> *Tommy John*

"You eat a lot of chicken because you don't know what the other meat is."

> *Barry Jones, on playing winter ball in the Dominican Republic*

"The menu listed it at market price. I didn't know that meant stock-market price."

> *Ron Kittle, on paying almost $50 for a lobster dinner*

"What I like best about baseball is the postgame spread in San Francisco."

Joe Magrane

"Improve my English quickly, because I don't want to eat hot dogs every day."

Martin Mainville, French-speaking player in the Expos farm system, on his goal for the year

"The only thing missing is there's no mustard in it."

Mickey Rivers, on the Reggie candy bars

"No thanks—I don't drink."

Jeff Stone, asked if he wanted a shrimp cocktail

FOOTBALL

"Baseball players are smarter than football players. How often do you see a baseball team penalized for too many men on the field?"

Jim Bouton

"You're the only pitcher I know who needs touchdowns instead of runs."

Roy Smalley, to Jerry Koosman after he lost two games in a row, 18–6 and 6–5

FOUL BALLS

"Why is the ball fair when it hits the foul pole?"
Larry Andersen

"It's a good thing it was seat cushion night."
Daryl Boston, on going into the stands to catch a foul ball

FREE AGENTS

"Everybody has heard about free-agent players. Well, we're a free-agent team."
Dave Righetti, on rumors that the Giants were going to St. Petersburg

"You pull up an old tree from the ground and move it, say, to California. Well, you can damage the roots."

Willie Stargell, on not becoming a free agent at the age of 40

"Not really—they lean toward cash."

Bill Veeck, on whether free agents leaned toward big cities

"I believe there are certain things that cannot be bought—loyalty, friendship, health, love, and an American League pennant."

Edward Bennett Williams, on why he refused to spend money on free agents

FUTURE

"Don't look back. Something may be gaining on you."

Satchel Paige

"I've seen the future, and it's much like the present, only longer."

Dan Quisenberry

GENERAL MANAGERS

"I don't care about being the youngest GM. I want to stick around to be the oldest."

Tom Grieve

"We didn't get a monkey off our back—we got a gorilla."

Charlie Kerfeld, after Dick Wagner resigned as the Astros general manager

GOLF

"It took me 17 years to get 3,000 hits. I did it in one afternoon on the golf course."

Hank Aaron

"Baseball reveals character; golf exposes it."

Ernie Banks

"I was three over: one over a house, one over a patio, and one over a swimming pool."

George Brett

"I hit one that far once—I did. And I still bogeyed the hole."

Ron Fairly, on a Mike Schmidt home run

"You're talking 70 and shooting 90."

Joe Frazier, talking loudly on the team bus to Tom Seaver, who was having an off year

"The safest place would be on the fairway."

Joe Garagiola, on the best place for the crowd to stand during a celebrity golf tournament

"I played golf with him a lot. Every time he threw a club, I picked it up. In a couple of weeks, I had a couple of sets."

Whitey Herzog, on Lee Thomas

"You can't call it a sport. You don't run, jump, you don't shoot, you don't pass. All you have to do is buy some clothes that don't match."

Steve Sax

"I tell myself that Jack Nicklaus probably has a lousy curveball."

Bob Walk, on not being a good golfer

GREAT GAMES

"I must admit, when Reggie hit his home run and I was sure nobody was looking, I applauded in my glove."

Steve Garvey, on Reggie Jackson's three home runs in Game 6 of the 1977 World Series

"I'm not what you call a real praying man, but out there I said to myself, 'Help me out, somebody.' "

Don Larsen, on his perfect game in the 1956 World Series

"Don Gullett is going to the Hall of Fame, and I'm going to the Eliot Lounge."

> *Bill Lee, after the Red Sox lost the seventh game of the 1975 World Series*

"I think there are going to be a lot of Reggies born in this town."

> *Bill Lee, after Jackson's three-home-run game*

GREATNESS

"There have been only two geniuses in the world— Willie Mays and William Shakespeare."
> *Tallulah Bankhead*

"He's the only guy I know who can go four for three."
> *Alan Bannister, on Rod Carew*

"Brooks never asked anyone to name a candy bar after him. In Baltimore, people name their children after him."

> *Gordon Beard, sportswriter, on Brooks Robinson*

"I can see how he won 25 games. What I don't understand is how he lost 5."

Yogi Berra, on Sandy Koufax

"You can't hit what you can't see."

Ping Bodie, on Walter Johnson

"I got a big charge out of seeing Ted Williams hit. Once in a while they let me try to field some of them, which sort of dimmed my enthusiasm."

Rocky Bridges

"During the reign of Hubbell, first base itself is a Marathon Route."

Heywood Broun, on Carl Hubbell

"Dickey wasn't just a catcher. He's a ball club."

Dan Daniel, sportswriter, on Bill Dickey

"If Satch and I were pitching on the same team, we'd clinch the pennant by July 4 and go fishing until the World Series."

Dizzy Dean, on Satchel Paige

"Babe Ruth wasn't born. The son of a bitch fell from a tree."

Joe Dugan

"George Brett could get good wood on an aspirin."
Jim Frey

"He could hit .300 with a fountain pen."
Joe Garagiola, on Stan Musial

"He enjoyed people enjoying themselves. He was color-blind and race-blind and religious-blind."
Hank Greenberg, on Bill Veeck

"I'd rather him pitch a crucial game for me drunk than anyone I've ever known sober. He was that good."
Rogers Hornsby, on Grover Cleveland Alexander

"When you call a pitcher 'Lefty' and everybody in both leagues knows who you mean, he must be pretty good."

Clint Hurdle, on Steve "Lefty" Carlton

"You used to think if the score was 5–0, he'd hit a five-run home run."

Reggie Jackson, on Willie Mays

"Blind people came to the park just to listen to him pitch."

Reggie Jackson, on Tom Seaver

"That's easy. You just take a gun and shoot him."

Ring Lardner, on the best way to stop Ty Cobb from hitting

"Every time I look at my pocketbook, I see Jackie Robinson."

Willie Mays

"Gibson's the luckiest pitcher I've ever seen because he always picks the night to pitch when the other team doesn't score any runs."

Tim McCarver, on Bob Gibson

"Everyone would like each other, and no one would get a hit."

Rance Mulliniks, asked what would happen if everyone in baseball was like Nolan Ryan

"Y is for Young. The Magnificent Cy. People batted against him. But I never knew why."
Ogden Nash

"The advantage of playing in New York is getting to watch Reggie Jackson play every day. And the disadvantage is in getting to watch Reggie Jackson play every day."
Graig Nettles

"Of what I saw of him, he was unhittable, unbelievable, and unthinkable."
Tom Paciorek, on Ron Guidry

"I hated McCarthy's guts, but there never was a better manager."
Joe Page, on Joe McCarthy

"If God had given him no balls and two strikes, he'd still get a hit."
Steve Palermo, on George Brett

"What does jelly do on peanut butter? That's what Junior means to us."
Bill Plummer, on what Ken Griffey, Jr., means to the Seattle Mariners

"He had me 0 and 2 before I ever got into the box."
Jerry Remy, on Jim Palmer

"The day Mickey Mantle bunted when the wind was blowing in on Crosley Field."
Robin Roberts, on his greatest All-Star Game thrill

"You saw him standing there, and you knew you had a pretty damn good chance to win the baseball game."
Red Ruffing, on Joe DiMaggio

"George Brett could roll out of bed on Christmas morning and hit a line drive."
John Schuerholz

"My hope for Nolan Ryan after he hangs up his spikes is to go to Harvard Med School. Not to study—to be studied."
Blackie Sherrod, sportswriter

"Ruth made a grave mistake when he gave up pitching. Working once a week, he might have lasted a long time and become a great star."

> *Indians player/manager Tris Speaker's 1921 comment on Babe Ruth's moving to the Yankees and becoming an outfielder*

"When Sandy Koufax retired."

> *Willie Stargell, on his greatest thrill in baseball*

"He was the best one-legged player I ever saw play the game."

> *Casey Stengel, on Mickey Mantle*

"Pardon me, Mr. Craig, but how are we going to defense Mr. McCovey—in the upper deck or lower deck?"

> *Casey Stengel to Roger Craig*

"A foul ball was a moral victory."

> *Don Sutton, on Sandy Koufax*

"It was like Frank Sinatra opening for Bob Uecker."

> *John Trautwein, on replacing Roger Clemens in a game*

"My boy, I can't recall anyone loading the bases against me."

> *Cy Young, being asked how he pitched with the bases loaded*

GREAT TEAMS

"You can never have too much talent. Even the 1927 Yankees didn't win every year."
Buzzie Bavasi

"Let's go out on the ballfield and hope we all don't get killed."

> *Donie Bush, Pirates manager, on facing the 1927 Yankees in the World Series*

"This might be a game of inches, but the Tigers have all the inches right now. They own the yardstick."

Bob Kearney, on the 1984 Detroit Tigers

"When the Mets lose a game, it's like William Perry losing eight pounds—who notices?"

Tim McCarver, on the 1986 Mets, who won their division by almost 20 games

HAIR

"On the mound is Randy Jones, the left-hander with a Karl Marx hairdo."

Jerry Coleman

"I still have it. I just keep it shaved."

Gary Gaetti, on his mustache

"I've been traveling so much I haven't had time to grow it."

Bob Horner, on not wearing a beard

"I call it the 'Watergate': I cover up everything I can."
Joe Torre, on his hairstyle

"I once grew a beard, and while I had it I slept at the north end of the bed and my wife slept at the south end. I finally shaved it, and we met at the equator."
Andy Van Slyke

HALL OF FAME

"I'm not proud. I'm willing to go in on my hands and knees if I have to."

> *Luke Appling, asked if he resented entering the Hall of Fame on the second ballot*

"Now I guess I'm 'mongst the mortals."

> *Dizzy Dean, on being inducted into the Hall of Fame*

"The Hall of Fame ceremonies are on the 31st and 32nd of July."

> *Ralph Kiner*

"Maybe 318 wins aren't enough. Maybe I'll have to go out and win some more games."

Phil Niekro, on not making it to the Hall of Fame in his first year of eligibility

"When I asked the baseball writers why they haven't elected me to the Hall of Fame, they told me they thought I was still playing."

Bob Uecker

"How did I feel when I heard the news? About the same way, I guess, that Columbus felt when he looked out from his ship and first saw land."

Dazzy Vance, on his induction into the Hall of Fame

HEIGHT

"Fred Patek was so small when he was born that his father passed out cigar butts."

Joey Adams, comedian

"We have baked potatoes in North Carolina that are bigger than him."

Greg Booker, on Bip Roberts

"He's so tall, he doesn't have a pickoff move. He just reaches out and tags the runner."

Rich Donnelly, Pirates third-base coach, on 6'10" pitcher Eric Hillman

"He's about 3'1". I tell him to get his nose off my kneecap."

Ron Luciano, on Earl Weaver

"Frank Howard is so big that he wasn't born; he was founded."

Jim Murray

HITTING

"When Manny takes a pitch, either it's a wild pitch or paralysis set in."

Joe Brown, on Manny Sanguillen

"I owe my success to expansion pitching, a short right-field fence, and my hollow bats."

Norm Cash

"Baseball is supposed to be a noncontact sport, but our hitters seem to be taking that literally."

Larry Doughty, Pirates GM

"I was a ball hitter. If I saw the ball, I hit it. If I didn't see it, I didn't hit it."

Ralph Garr

"What we could use is a couple of shutouts, but I don't know if that would be good enough to win."

Whitey Herzog, on a weak-hitting St. Louis Cardinals team

"We're like a soccer team—if we're two down, we're dead."

Whitey Herzog, on that same Cardinals team

"Can you believe it? They sent me a whole shipment of bats and not one set of directions."

Steve Lake, on hitting .141

"They couldn't break a chandelier if they held batting practice in a hotel lobby."

Bill Lee, on the California Angels

"Anybody who can't get along with a .400 hitter is crazy."

Joe McCarthy, on Ted Williams

"Basically, I had things on my side because I know how stupid hitters are."

Jim Morrison, infielder, on pitching a scoreless inning

"I can hit any pitcher alive—if he stands still."

Richie Scheinblum

"They give you a round bat, and they throw you a round ball. And they tell you to hit it square."

Willie Stargell

"All I want out of life is when I walk down the street folks will say, 'There goes the greatest hitter who ever lived.' "

Ted Williams

HITTING PITCHERS

"I'm seeing the ball real good. I just can't hit it."
Don Carman, asked if he was seeing the ball well when hitting .024

"Even a blind dog finds a bone every once in a while."
Bruce Hurst, on his first major league hit

HITTING STREAKS

"If Rose's streak were still intact, with that single to left, the fans would be throwing babies out of the upper deck."
Jerry Coleman

"If I tell, everybody will do it, and we'll be out there for five hours, but nobody will get anybody out."
Rick Dempsey, on not giving the secret to his hitting streak

"I'm superstitious, and every night after I got a hit, I ate Chinese food and drank tequila. I had to stop hitting or die."

Tim Flannery, on a hitting streak

"This isn't a salary drive—it's a survival drive."

Jamie Quirk, on being on a hitting streak

HOME RUNS

"They picked that up on the radar screen in Red Square."

Mike Bielecki, on Pedro Guerrero hitting a 425-foot homer off him

"It's pretty bad when your family asks for passes to the game and wants to sit in the left-field bleachers."

Bert Blyleven, on the possibility that he would break his own record of allowing the most home runs in a season

"It really wasn't dramatic. No little boy in the hospital asked me to hit one. I didn't promise it to my kid for his birthday, and my wife will be too shocked to appreciate it."

> *Rocky Bridges, on his first home run in two seasons*

"I've always thought that if you hit the second deck, it should be two runs. Fifth deck, that's it—game over."

> *Jose Canseco*

"They usually show movies on a flight like that."

> *Ken Coleman, announcer, on a long Bob Watson home run*

"The last time I hit a home run in the bottom of the ninth to win a game was in Strat-O-Matic."

> *Len Dykstra, on hitting a game-winning home run in the bottom of the ninth to win Game 3 of the 1986 playoffs for the Mets*

"I wanted to go into my home-run trot, but I realized I didn't have one."

> *Jim Essian, hitting his first home run in more than 100 games*

"Never has a home run been so anonymous."

*Steve Garvey, on hitting a home run
while an attractive woman was parading around the stands*

"When Neil Armstrong set foot on the moon, he found six baseballs that Jimmie Foxx hit off me in 1937."

Lefty Gomez

"I looked in my glove and then on the ground. That left only one place—the other side of the fence."

Pat Kelly, on a home run by Roy Smalley

"Home-run hitters drive Cadillacs; singles hitters drive Fords."

Ralph Kiner

"Some of our guys would have to pick the ball up and hit it three times to get it that far."

Steve McCatty, on a 450-foot home run by Bruce Bochte

"The home run is sort of like a dunk in basketball. When you do it, everyone notices. And when you don't, everyone notices."

Cal Ripken

"I've given up many a thrill in my career."

Frank Tanana, on giving up Joe Carter's first home run

INDIANS

"Our own."

Peter Bavasi, Indians president, on the team he fears the most

"I'm not used to being funny and cracking jokes like everyone else is doing. In Cleveland, we took our banquets seriously and saved the jokes for the game."

Von Hayes, speaking at a banquet after being traded by the Indians

"The first thing they do in Cleveland if you have talent is trade you for three guys who don't."

Jim Kern

"If they had 75,000 fans in Cleveland for the opener, they must have passed out 300,000 free tickets."
Graig Nettles

"The best thing about playing in Cleveland is that you don't have to make road trips there."
Richie Scheinblum

INDOOR STADIUMS

"Playing indoors reminds me of when I was a kid and you had to go to your room and you couldn't go outside. It was like you were being punished."
George Brett

INJURIES

"It wasn't my arm. It was my forearm."
Joaquin Andujar

"Back then, if you had a sore arm, the only people concerned were you and your wife. Now it's you, your wife, your agent, your investment counselor, your stockbroker, and your publisher."

Jim Bouton

"I'm like Rice Krispies—snap, crackle, pop."

Jack Clark, on his injured knees

"It's an old foot."

Charlie Hough, on why his foot didn't swell after it was hit by a line drive

"I always said I wanted to lead by example, but this is ridiculous."

Ken Howell, first of nine Phillies to go on the disabled list in one season

"I've had so many X-rays that my pitches might take on a subtle glow."

Joe Magrane

"Ice is for mixed drinks."

Warren Spahn, asked if he put ice on a sore arm

"Because 85 percent of the fans have artificial hips."

Robin Ventura, on why Bo Jackson received a standing ovation in a spring training game in Sarasota, Florida

"I never had any quads when I played."

Dick Williams, on Spike Owen's injured quads

INSULTS

"All I'd have to do is make my head look like a slider and he'd miss it by six inches."

Jim Colborn, on Aurelio Rodriguez threatening to hit him on the head with his bat

"Some people who don't say *ain't* ain't eating."

Dizzy Dean, responding to criticism of his grammar

"Five runs ahead and he'd knock in all the runs I could ask for. One run behind and he was going to kill me."

Leo Durocher, on Ron Santo

"He doesn't have ulcers. But he's one of the biggest carriers there is."

Jim Fregosi, on Mitch Williams

"I heard that Bill Buckner tried to commit suicide over the winter. He stepped in front of a car, but it went through his legs."

Billy Gardner, on Bill Buckner's error in the sixth game of the 1986 World Series

"He likes to complain about not playing, which is what he does best—not play."

Pat Gillick, on Mike Marshall

"Moe Berg could speak eight languages, but he couldn't hit in any of them."

Ted Lyons, on the well-educated Berg

"Maybe two Young Awards should be presented each year—the Cy for the best pitcher and the Anthony for the worst."

> *Allan Malamud, sportswriter, on Anthony Young, who lost 27 straight games*

"When Charlie Finley had his heart operation, it took eight hours—seven just to find his heart."
> *Steve McCatty*

"Let's be serious. How many clubs call for Kurt Bevacqua."

> *Jack McKeon, asked if any contenders wanted Bevacqua*

"Some people have a chip on their shoulders. Billy has a whole lumberyard."
> *Jim Murray, on Billy Martin*

"His limitations are limitless."
> *Danny Ozark, on Mike Anderson*

"Son, we'd like to keep you around this season, but we're going to try to win a pennant."

> *Casey Stengel, on cutting Aubrey Gatewood*

"He's the only man I know Dale Carnegie would hit in the mouth."

> *Bill Veeck, on Walter O'Malley*

INTELLIGENCE

"It puzzles me how they know what corners are good for filling stations. Just how did these fellows know there was gas and oil under there?"

> *Dizzy Dean*

"The Good Lord was good to me. He gave me a strong body, a good right arm, and a weak mind."

> *Dizzy Dean*

"I'm in the best shape of my life, and that includes my brain."

> *Len Dykstra*

"Albert Einstein was bad in English. Of course, Einstein was German."

> *Bob Kearney, defending his own intelligence*

"The kid is the greatest proof of reincarnation. Nobody could get that stupid in one lifetime."

> *Joe McCarthy, after a player was thrown out trying to steal home with one out*

"I have no trouble with the 12 inches between my elbow and my palm. It's the seven inches between my ears that's bent."

> *Tug McGraw*

"I'll tell you how smart Pete is. When they had the blackout in New York, he was stranded 13 hours on an escalator."

> *Joe Nuxhall, on Pete Rose*

"We told him to learn from the past, but forget about it."

> *Lou Piniella, on the frequently injured Chris Brown*

"Out of what—a thousand?"

Mickey Rivers, on Reggie Jackson's claim that he had a 160 IQ

"He is the first pitcher to make the major leagues with one brain cell."

Roy Smalley, on Mickey Hatcher

"You should forget about those big words. You can't get 'em out in the library."

Casey Stengel, on pitcher Jay Hook, who had a genius IQ

INTENTIONAL WALKS

"Get an intentional walk."

Nolan Ryan, asked if there was anything in baseball that he had never done

"I was such a dangerous hitter; I even got intentional walks in batting practice."

Casey Stengel, on his playing days

"An hour after the game, you want to go out and play them again."

Rocky Bridges

"The motto of the team I played for was 'win or else.' I didn't know what the 'else' meant, and I never wanted to learn."

Chuck Cary

"Cecil Fielder may be the only Japanese import ever to be cheered in Detroit."

Don Criqui

"I like Doug DeCinces and all, but I got tired of talking to him all the time."

Terry Harper, on the loneliness of playing in Japan

"I should be hungry, but I've already had breakfast and lunch tomorrow."

Whitey Herzog, on a flight back from Japan

"If the money was right, I could live on Alpo for eight months."

> *Reggie Jackson, on the possibility of playing in Japan*

"It took us 35 years to get revenge for Pearl Harbor."

> *Vin Scully, on Leo Durocher managing a Japanese team in 1976*

JEWELRY

"I'm a David, and I'm a star."

> *Dave Parker, on why he wears a Star of David*

JOBS

"I never heard of anybody getting a job they applied for."

> *Gene Lamont, on not applying for a managerial job*

"It gets more exciting every year, but I wish they'd give me something to do."

> Stan Musial, on being a VP of the Cardinals

"I ain't ever had a job. I just always played baseball."

> Satchel Paige

JUICED-UP BASEBALLS

"My 10-hop singles are getting through the infield on 8 hops."

> Dave Collins

"Since the overthrow of the government, the workers are happier and they're doing a better job."

> Gary Gaetti, on the lively baseballs coming from Haiti

"We won't have to buy balls this year. We just put them in the ball bag and let them multiply."

> Chuck Hartenstein

KNOCKDOWNS

"The trick against Drysdale is to hit him before he hits you."

Orlando Cepeda

KNUCKLEBALLS

"A stadium with the lights out."

Charlie Hough, on the best situation for a knuckleball pitcher

"It actually giggles at you as it goes by you."

Rick Monday, on Phil Niekro's knuckler

"Trying to hit him is like trying to eat Jell-O with chopsticks."

Bobby Murcer, on knuckleballer Phil Niekro

"I'd have a better chance of catching flies with Chinese chopsticks."

> *Andy Van Slyke, on Tim Wakefield's knuckleball*

"Now I'll see if I can control a few knuckleheads."

> *Hoyt Wilhelm, on going from being baseball's top knuckleball pitcher to being a minor league manager*

LEFTIES

"What do you expect in a northpaw world?"

> *Bill Lee, on why lefties are always flaky*

"We left-handers feel we're the only ones in our right mind."

> *Greg Mathews*

LEGENDS

"Yeah, what paper you write for, Ernie?"
> *Yogi Berra, on being introduced to writer Ernest Hemingway*

"Some twenty years ago, I stopped talking about Babe for the simple reason that I realized that those who had never seen him didn't believe me."
> *Tommy Holmes, on Babe Ruth*

"We gave all the other guys gas money. We gave him covered-wagon money."
> *Doug Melvin, Orioles assistant GM, on 36-year-old minor leaguer Daniel Boone*

LITTLE LEAGUE

"I think it's all right; it keeps the parents off the streets."
> *Rocky Bridges*

"How can a guy win a game if you don't give him any runs?"

Bo Belinsky, after losing a game 15–0

"If a tie is like kissing your sister, losing is like kissing your grandmother with her teeth out."

George Brett

"I think I get more upset when I lose a fish. In baseball, there's always another game tomorrow, another chance to be a hero. That's not true with a big fish."

Ron Davis

"We had a case of Ripple on ice."

John Felske, on the Phillies making it to second place at the end of the season

"Well, I haven't lost a game for a long time."

Whitey Herzog, on how he felt about being out of baseball for a year

"It's like Noah's wife told him—'Noah, honey, it's going to stop raining one of these days.' "

Mike Krukow, on losing a game 21–3

"I'd hate to be on a team that goes down in history with the '64 Phillies and the '67 Arabs."

Bill Lee, on the '78 Red Sox losing a 14-game lead to the Yankees

"We were as flat tonight as people used to think the earth was."

Danny Ozark

"We're fine. The only time we lose our concentration is when the umpire says, 'Play ball.' "

Lou Piniella, asked if his team was mentally prepared

LOSING STREAKS

"I've heard of guys going 0 for 15 or 0 for 25, but I was 0 for July."

Bob Aspromonte

"We lost 13 straight one year. I decided if we got rained out, we'd have a victory party."

Lefty Gomez, on managing in the minors

"It was not like we had a monkey on our back—it was more like Godzilla."

Fred Lynn, on the Orioles ending a long losing streak

"It doesn't bother him. All he cares about after the game is getting in line for a Snow-Kone."

Al Newman, on his nine-year-old son's reaction to a Twins losing streak

"I'm taking antihistamines and antidepressants."

Tom Trebelhorn, on developing allergies during a long losing streak

"That wasn't even a big monkey that was on my back. It was a zoo."

Anthony Young, on winning a game after losing 27 straight

LOTTERY

"I feel like I just struck out Joe DiMaggio with the bases loaded and two outs in the ninth."

>*Mickey McDermott, on his wife winning $6 million in the Arizona lottery*

"She is now."

>*Chuck Tanner, asked if his aunt who won $2.5 million in the lottery was his favorite*

LOYALTY

"You have pets for loyalty."

>*Wade Boggs, on his loyalty being questioned when he left the Red Sox for the Yankees*

"I changed the felt on my pool table to red and the rug in the family room to blue. If I switched team colors, I would have had to redo the whole house."

>*Kent Hrbek, on staying loyal to the Twins*

MALAPROPS AND
FRACTURED SYNTAX

"America has one word that says it all: 'You never know.' "

>Joaquin Andujar

"Yeah, only in America can a thing like this happen."

>Yogi Berra, on a Jewish mayor being
>elected in Dublin, Ireland

"That's his style of hitting. If you can't imitate him, don't copy him."

>Yogi Berra

"Get me a diet Tab."

>Yogi Berra

"No, but he did a lot better than I thought he would."

>Yogi Berra, on whether Don Mattingly
>exceeded expectations

"McCovey swings and misses, and it's fouled back."
Jerry Coleman

"Rich Folkers is throwing up in the bullpen."
Jerry Coleman

"George Hendrick simply lost that sun-blown pop-up."
Jerry Coleman

"There's a hard shot at LeMaster, and he throws Madlock into the dugout."
Jerry Coleman

"Enos Cabell started out with the Astros. And before that he was with the Orioles."
Jerry Coleman

"Next up is Fernando Gonzales—who is not playing tonight."
Jerry Coleman

"Gaylord Perry and Willie McCovey should know each other like a book. They've been ex-teammates for years now."
Jerry Coleman

"We're all sad to see Glenn Beckert leave. Before he goes, though, I hope he stops by so we can kiss him good-bye. He's that kind of guy."

Jerry Coleman

"Old Diz knows the king's English. And not only that, I also know the queen is English."

Dizzy Dean, defending his grammar

"He takes a bunt for a called third strike."

Ron Fairly

"The Giants are looking for a trade, but I don't think Atlanta wants to depart with a quality player."

Ron Fairly

"Last night I neglected to mention something that bears repeating."

Ron Fairly

"I mostly stayed around the house. But I did take a hunting trip to one of those Canadian proverbs."

Jim Gantner, on his vacation

"I must have had ambrosia."

>*Jim Gantner, on missing a radio show appearance*

"It wasn't bad, but we had to use contemporary greens."

>*Jim Gantner, on golf*

"Buenos Dias."

>*Jim Gantner, when asked the capital of Argentina*

"It's only puffy when it's swollen."

>*Charlie Hough, on a broken finger*

"It's permanent, for now."

>*Roberto Kelly, on changing his name to Bobby*

"It's our season of destination."

>*Charlie Kerfeld, on a great season for Houston*

"Rookie Wilson was candidate for Mookie of the Year."

Ralph Kiner

"Third base is certainly a reactionary position."

Ralph Kiner

"All the Mets' road wins against Los Angeles this year have been at Dodger Stadium."

Ralph Kiner

"The Mets have gotten their leadoff hitter on base only once in this inning."

Ralph Kiner

"They will pass the father-son tandem of Buddy Bell and Yogi Berra."

Ralph Kiner, on Bobby and Barry Bonds becoming the all-time father-son home-run leaders

"We're going to hang our heads high."

Harvey Kuenn, after the Brewers lost the '82 World Series

"I'll have a pie à la mode with ice cream."
Johnny Logan

"I know the name but I can't replace the face."
Johnny Logan

"Rome wasn't born in a day."
Johnny Logan

"I'll have to go with the immoral Babe Ruth."
Johnny Logan, asked to name the greatest player of all-time

"I will perish this trophy forever."
Johnny Logan

"Maybe I can find some major league suspects."
Johnny Logan, on doing some scouting

"No longer than that. Maybe a month and a half."
Junior Ortiz, on being asked if an injury would keep him out for six weeks

"I remember a lot of things. I just can't remember them."

> *Junior Ortiz, on memories of five years with the Pirates*

"Hey, cabbie, could you turn that thing down a hundred disciples?"

> *Paul Owens, on a loud radio*

"You can lead a horse to water, but you can't stick his head in it."

> *Paul Owens*

"Even Napoleon had his Watergate."

> *Danny Ozark*

"My jobs are to hit .300, score 100 runs, and stay injury prone."

> *Mickey Rivers*

"It could permanently hurt a batter for a long time."

> *Pete Rose*

"I just talked to the doctor. He told me her contraptions were an hour apart."

> *Mackey Sasser, on his wife's pregnancy*

"All right, everyone line up alphabetically according to your height."

> *Casey Stengel*

MANAGING

"He doesn't have to march to the same drummer as long as he's in the same band."

> *Dusty Baker, on managing Barry Bonds*

"There are three things the average man thinks he can do better than everybody else: build a fire, run a motel, and manage a baseball team."

> *Rocky Bridges*

"Between owners and players, a manager today has become a wishbone."

> *John Curtis*

"If you're looking for job security, drive a mail truck. Managers always get fired."
> *Alvin Dark*

"Once a man begins managing, his age should be calculated like a dog's—one year equals seven human years."
> *Nick Leyva*

"I miss innings one through nine, but not Cleveland or Detroit."
> *Gene Mauch, asked if he missed managing*

"I think they recycle more managers than cans."
> *Billy North*

"The toughest thing about managing is standing up for nine innings."
> *Paul Owens*

"I was the smartest manager I ever played for."
> *Pete Rose, on being asked who was the greatest manager he ever played for*

"A manager is like a fellow swimming in the ocean with a cut on his arm. Sooner or later the sharks are going to get him."

Eddie Stanky

"The secret of managing a club is to keep the five guys who hate you from the five who are undecided."

Casey Stengel

"If he had made me a consultant five minutes ago, my first recommendation would have been not to fire the manager."

John Wathan, on being offered a job as a consultant after being fired by the Royals

MARINERS

"Noah."

Barry Bonnell, former Seattle Mariner, when asked who his all-time favorite Mariner was

MARLINS

"Are you kidding? The way they boo me here, they'd be throwing hand grenades at me over there."

> *Jose Canseco, on speculation that he would be traded to the Florida Marlins, his hometown team*

MARRIAGE

"No one is a pull hitter in the first year of marriage."
> *Walker Cooper*

"It was better than rooming with Joe Page."
> *Joe DiMaggio, asked if being married to Marilyn Monroe was good for him*

"We've been married 28 years, and we still go out dining and dancing three times a week. She goes on Mondays, Wednesdays, and Fridays; I go on Tuesdays, Thursdays, and Saturdays."
> *Tommy Lasorda*

"No, sir, but I'm in great demand."

Satchel Paige, asked if he was married

"Guys are trying to get married . . . or unmarried."

Dan Quisenberry, on why some play-
ers take binoculars to the bullpen
with them

"I always said I gave Mike Cuellar more chances than I gave my first wife."

Earl Weaver

MEDIOCRITY

"I'm going to play with harder nonchalance this year."

Jackie Brandt

"The more I played with them, the more I found that no one could take a joke—my batting average."

Rocky Bridges, on batting .237 for the
Dodgers

"The only thing standing between Jack Perconte and an outstanding major league career is performance."
Del Crandall

"In baseball there are only two things I'm an expert in—trades and slumps."
Joe Garagiola

"Baseball has been good to me since I quit trying to play it."
Whitey Herzog

"The Dodgers are such a .500 club, they could probably split a three-game series."
Vin Scully

"I've had many years that I was not so successful as a ballplayer, as it was a game of skill."
Casey Stengel

"I'm in the twilight of a mediocre career."
Frank Sullivan

"I made a major contribution to the Cardinals' pennant drive in 1964. I got hepatitis."
Bob Uecker

"It isn't the high price of stars that is expensive; it's the high price of mediocrity."
Bill Veeck

METRODOME

"I don't think there are good uses for nuclear weapons, but this place might be one."
Dan Quisenberry

METS

"I hate the New York Mets more than I hate Communists. At least Communists don't have off-season problems."
Bill Murray

"Not a bit; we lose at any altitude."

> *Casey Stengel, asked if the altitude had contributed to the Mets' loss of an exhibition game in Mexico City*

"Our first Mets game was April 10, 1962. And it was our best game. It was rained out."

> *Casey Stengel*

MICROWAVES

"I can always catch a couple of hours of sleep in front of it—and it takes me only three minutes."

> *Sparky Anderson*

"Everything went all right until I put their socks in the microwave to dry."

> *Sammy Stewart, on spending a day taking care of his kids*

"I'm trying not to put too much pressure on myself, but I think I'm overcompensating. I'm putting too much pressure on myself not to put too much pressure on myself."

>*Dann Bilardello, on being sent to the minors*

"I took one giant step backwards."

>*Rocky Bridges, on moving from Triple-A ball to A ball*

"I hate the minor leagues. I'd rather go out to lunch with my ex-wife's attorney than play in the minors."

>*Dave Collins*

"What makes it bad is that I was looking forward to the three days off."

>*Chili Davis, on being sent to the minors just a few days before the all-star break*

"The grass is greener, the sun's not as hot, and the dirt is not as dirty."

> *Bobby Dues, minor league ballplayer, on the difference between the majors and the minors*

"Pawtucket is a much bigger city on the way up than it is on the way down."

> *Glenn Hoffman, on the Red Sox sending him to Pawtucket*

"It was easy . . . meal money in the Southern League was $13 a day."

> *Charles Kerfeld, on losing 30 pounds in the minors*

"I'd rather ride the buses managing in Triple A than be a lawyer."

> *Tony LaRussa, manager and attorney*

"I know I'm not in the major leagues."

> *Scotti Madison, asked if he knew where he was when he had a concussion three days after being sent to the minors*

"Where would you rather start the season, Syracuse or Las Vegas?"

> *Luis Salazar, on why he signed a minor league contract with the Padres and not the Blue Jays*

"Waking up this morning in the Ritz Carlton felt pretty good. It's not the Holiday Inn."

> *Doug Saunders, Mets rookie, on being called up to the majors*

"No one will survive that many buses."

> *Stan Wasiak, asked if his record for most wins by a minor league manager would ever be surpassed*

MONEY

"If the guy was real poor, I'd give it back to him."

> *Yogi Berra, asked what he would do if he found a million dollars*

"Rickey had both money and players. He just didn't like to see the two of them mix."

Chuck Connors, on Branch Rickey

"Ballplayers and deer hunters are alike. They both want the big bucks."

Larry Doughty, Pirates GM

"I can't imagine making all that money and not having the time to spend it."

John Elway, on Bo Jackson when he played both football and baseball

"If they put a lien against us, I've got a couple of pitchers they can have."

Billy Gardner, on plans by Minneapolis to assess property tax against the Twins' stadium

"Isn't it amazing that we're worth so much on the trading block and worth so little when we talk salary with the general manager?"

Jim Kern

"I had no idea it was worth $50,000. If I did, I'd be sleeping in it."

> *Mickey Mantle, on his jersey being sold for $50,000*

"With the money I'm making, I should be playing two positions."

> *Pete Rose*

"I know, but I had a better year than Hoover."

> *Babe Ruth, when a reporter pointed out that his 1930 salary of $80,000 was higher than the president's $75,000*

"He'd go into the vault to get a nickel change."

> *Enos Slaughter, on Branch Rickey*

"You can have money stacked to the ceiling, but the size of your funeral is still going to depend upon the weather."

> *Chuck Tanner*

"You know I signed with the Milwaukee Braves for $3,000. That bothered my dad at the time, because he didn't have that kind of dough to pay out. But eventually he scraped it up."

Bob Uecker

"They throw money at us—quarters, nickels. Why? Throw me a tax audit. Throw me your electric bill."

Andy Van Slyke, on fans throwing things at players

"In here, it ought to be 'W-4 million' forms."

Andy Van Slyke, on W-4 tax forms being passed around the Pirates' clubhouse

"I felt like one of those instant millionaires."

Harry Walker, after signing for a $2,500 bonus in 1939

MOTHERS

"When I played baseball, I got death threats all the time—from my mother."
> *Bob Uecker*

"Good mothers are underrated, just like good defense."
> *Andy Van Slyke*

MOVIES

"He must have done that one before he died."
> *Yogi Berra, on seeing Steve McQueen*
> *in* The Magnificent Seven

"Jeez. They're going to give me 50,000 smackers just for living."
> *Dizzy Dean, on a movie about his life*

"I looked at his pass list and asked him if it was the cast from *Deliverance*."

> *Tim Flannery, on John Kruk's family coming to a game from his small hometown in West Virginia*

"Well, she's already had so much experience grabbing herself, she should be great."

> *Jay Leno, on Madonna appearing in the movie* A League of Their Own

"I've played in more towns than *Gone With the Wind*."

> *Frank Lucchesi, on his many managerial changes*

"I couldn't have driven Miss Daisy home today."

> *Andy Van Slyke, after a bad day at the plate*

"Gee, you've known me all these years and still don't know how to spell my name."

> *Yogi Berra, after receiving a check that said "Payable to Bearer"*

"I was hopin' he wouldn't get a hit so I didn't have to pronounce their names."

> *Dizzy Dean, on the batter coming to the plate with the bases loaded: Kluszewski on first, Borkowski on second, and Baczewski on third*

"I can't remember your name. But I know we used to pitch you high and outside."

> *Bill Dickey, asked by Joe Gantenbein if Dickey remembered him*

"I told Roland to go out and get me a big-name pitcher. He said Wehrmeister's got 11 letters. Is that a big enough name for me?"

> *Eddie Einhorn, after White Sox GM Roland Hemond acquired Dave Wehrmeister*

"I picked up the paper and said, 'Gee, we got Butler.' Quinton [six-year-old son] said, 'Why do we need a butler? We already have a live-in.'"

Orel Hershiser, on Brett Butler's acquisition by the Dodgers

"Don Bordello is coming up to the plate."

Ralph Kiner, mispronouncing Dann Bilardello

"We both have a Henderson problem."

Tony LaRussa, to Bobby Knight, referring to Rickey Henderson after Knight's star player Alan Henderson was injured

"I don't play Mike Scioscia because he's Italian; I play him because I'm Italian."

Tommy Lasorda

"I'm always up in the bullpen just in case they need me."

Dave Leiper, relief pitcher, on why he named his son Justin Casey

"I couldn't pronounce it myself."

> *Bob Miller, on changing his name from Gmeinweiser*

"John Smiley is going to change his name to John Frowny."

> *Tony Perez, on reports that John Smiley was unhappy about being traded from Pittsburgh to Minnesota*

"He's the least impressive Chamberlain since Neville."

> *Vin Scully, on Wes Chamberlain*

"Who would you rather be? Wee Willie or Big Dave?"

> *Dave Winfield, on passing Wee Willie Keeler on the all-time hit list*

"Nobody told me there'd be Daves like this."

> *Dave Winfield, on what opposing pitchers must be saying when they face Winfield and Dave Parker batting next to each other in the Angels' lineup*

NATIONAL ANTHEM

"Most of us have such bad voices, we respect the national anthem by not singing it."
                    Sparky Anderson

"It'll be great not to have to listen to two different national anthems."
                    *Mitch Webster, on being traded away
                    from the Expos*

NEWSPAPERS

"The only thing I read in the paper is the comics. When they start mixing the sports with the comics, I'll stop getting my subscription."
                    Bo Jackson

"Now I know why Ralph Kramden was in a bad mood all the time."

Jim Deshaies, on the Astros' bus taking an hour and a half to go a short distance to Shea Stadium

"I could never play in New York. The first time I ever came into a game there, I got into the bullpen cart and they told me to lock the door."
Mike Flanagan

"That borough of churches and bad ball clubs, many of which I had."
Casey Stengel, on Brooklyn

NIGHTMARES

" 'Sorry, Mickey,' the Lord said, 'but I wanted to give you the word personally. You can't go to heaven because of the way you acted down on earth, but do you mind signing a dozen baseballs?' "

Mickey Mantle, on a recurring nightmare

NO-HITTERS

"If I'd known I was gonna pitch a no-hitter, I would have gotten a haircut."

Bo Belinsky

"It couldn't have happened to a greater guy. Well, yes it could. It could have happened to me."

Tommy Lasorda, on Jerry Reuss pitching a no-hitter

"Well, there goes our 26-game hitting streak."

John McNamara, on Jim Palmer throwing a no-hitter against the A's in 1969

NUMBERS

"You give 100 percent in the first half of the game, and if that isn't enough, in the second half you give what's left."

Yogi Berra

"Better make it four. I don't think I can eat eight."

Yogi Berra, asked if he wanted his pizza cut into four or eight slices

"We talked five times. I called him twice, and he called me twice."

Larry Bowa, on off-season conversations with Stan Jefferson

"You can count on the fingers of your right hand the number of times I've hit a homer to the opposite field. About 10."

Gary Carter

"So the Padres take a three-game series from the Giants, three games to two."

Jerry Coleman

"Nobody should be 4–1, unless it's the '27 Yankees, and they're too old."

Whitey Herzog, on the '88 Mets being 4–1 favorites to win the World Series

"Two grand slams in a week—man, that's seven or eight ribbies right there."

Bill Madlock, on Al Oliver

"He told the pitchers to pair off in threes."

Mickey Mantle, recounting a Yogi Berra story

"Me and George and Billy are two of a kind."

Mickey Rivers, on his relationship with Billy Martin and George Steinbrenner

"Ninety percent of the game is half mental."
Jim Wohlford

"It could just as easily have gone the other way."
Don Zimmer, after the Cubs went 4–4 on a road trip

OAKLAND A'S

"Was it difficult leaving the *Titanic*?"
Sal Bando, on leaving the Oakland A's during Charles Finley's reign

"We run our club like a pawn shop—we buy, we trade, we sell."
Charles Finley

"I couldn't play when I played."
> *Sparky Anderson, on why he didn't participate in a Tigers Old-Timers game*

"I'm sure glad the season is over."
> *Luke Appling, hitting a home run at the age of 75 in an Old-Timers Game*

"The real thrill in this game is to finish it."
> *Lou Brock, playing in an Old-Timers Game*

"Old-Timers Games, weekends, and airplane landings are alike. If you can walk away from them, they're successful."
> *Casey Stengel*

"We're getting close to Opening Day—I don't know if that's good or bad."

> *Sparky Anderson, on prospects for the*
> *'93 Tigers*

"A home opener is always exciting, no matter if it's home or on the road."

> *Yogi Berra*

"Admiral Byrd threw out the first ball."

> *Rocky Bridges, on a cold Opening Day*
> *in Buffalo*

"He tried to burn it in there. I decided the main thing was to get it to the catcher."

> *President Clinton, comparing his*
> *opening day lob to the poor throw of*
> *President Bush the year before*

"No, I'm not excited. It's no big deal. How the hell is a man my age going to get excited?"

> *Joe Frazier, former Mets manager, on*
> *Opening Day at 53*

"It's like Christmas, except it's warmer."
Pete Rose

ORIOLES

"Baltimore's such a lousy town. Francis Scott Key went out in a boat to write 'The Star-Spangled Banner.' "
Billy Martin

"A great place to go if you're a crab."
Jim Murray, on Baltimore

"I'm having a communications problem with the Orioles. I can't seem to communicate to them that I'm a good pitcher."

Chris Welsh, on having a 23.64 ERA against Baltimore and a 2.70 ERA against the rest of the league

"There's nothing in the world I wouldn't do for them. And there's nothing they wouldn't do for me. That's the way it is—we go through life doing nothing for each other."

> *Gene Autry, Angels owner, on his relationship with the Dodgers*

"My position is that while the players don't deserve all that money, the owners don't deserve it even more."
> *Jim Bouton*

"I'm going to write a book—*How to Make a Small Fortune in Baseball.* You start with a large fortune."
> *Ruly Carpenter, Phillies president*

"I heard he's so rich, he bought his dog a boy."
> *Billy Gardner, on Twins owner Carl Pohlad*

"I bought the Braves for two reasons—to get an autographed baseball without pleading for it and to get good seats."
> *Ted Turner*

"The dumbest NFL owner is equal to the smartest baseball owner."

Edward Bennett Williams

PAIN

"Pain don't hurt."

Sparky Anderson

"If the human body recognized agony and frustration, people would never run marathons, have babies, or play baseball."

Carlton Fisk

PENNANT RACES

"Just give me 25 guys on the last year of their contract; I'll win a pennant every year."

Sparky Anderson

"We're like tea bags. The flavor doesn't come out until you put us in hot water."

>Mike Davis, on how long it took the A's to get into the pennant race

"September is panty-hose month: no nonsense."

>Dave Parker

PHILLIES

"That's too bad; they're the only team I can beat."

>Dave Cole, on being traded to the Phillies in the mid-1950s

"You know how it is. If we win it, it's because we're a veteran team. If we lose it, it's because we're too old."

>Mike Schmidt, on an aging Phillies team

"Philadelphia is the only city in the world where you can experience the thrill of victory and the agony of reading about it the next day."

>Mike Schmidt

"Phillies fans would boo a wake."
Joe Dugan

"Some of these people would boo the crack in the Liberty Bell."
Pete Rose

"You know what they do when the game's rained out? They go to the airport and boo landings."
Bob Uecker

"When there was an Easter egg hunt before a game in Connie Mack Stadium, there would be a few kids who couldn't find any eggs. The crowd would boo them."
Bob Uecker

PIRATES

"With the Cardinals I'd come in and find everyone reading the stock market report. With the Pirates I come in and find everyone reading the papers to see if Hulk Hogan won."

Andy Van Slyke

PITCHING

"When I started to throw the ball back to the pitcher harder than he was throwing it to me, we changed positions."

Bert Blyleven

"You've got to remember—I'm 73."

Ty Cobb, on why he felt he could hit only .300 against modern pitching

"You don't save a pitcher for tomorrow. Tomorrow it may rain."

Leo Durocher

"Our earned run average looks like the national debt."

Charlie Fox, Giants manager, 1973

"I was never nervous when I had the ball, but when I let it go I was scared to death."

Lefty Gomez

"I made some dumb pitches when I had to."

Dave LaPoint, explaining why he lost a game

"I'm the greatest 60-foot pitcher in baseball. If I can conquer those last 6 inches, I'll be on my way."

Barry Latman

"I've seen guys pitch bad, and I've seen guys pitch in bad luck, but you've done an outstanding job of putting it all together."

Sparky Lyle, to Jim Kern

"I was afraid I might strangle him if I had him in the dugout."

Gene Mauch, on why he let Pete Redfern pitch badly for several innings rather than take him out of the game

156

"I get in a windup and make something up as I go along."

Dale Mohorcic, on why he varies his pitching delivery

"The only thing wrong with our pitchers is they all have to pitch the same night."

Don Osborn, former Pirates pitching coach

"The batter still hits a grounder. But in this case the first bounce is 360 feet away."

Dan Quisenberry, on what happens when his sinker doesn't work

"He has wonderful stuff and wonderful control and throws strikes, which shows he's educated. But then, say you're educated and you can't throw strikes. Then they don't leave you in too long."

Casey Stengel, on Mike Marshall

"Not true at all. Vaseline is manufactured right here in the United States."

Don Sutton, on accusations that he doctors the baseball with foreign substances

"I pitch like my hair's on fire."
Mitch Williams

PLATOONING

"He could manage against righties, and I could manage against lefties."

> *Garth Iorg, manager at Knoxville, after Rance Mulliniks was sent down. Both players used to platoon with each other at third base for Toronto*

POLITICS

"He sat right where I usually sit. I didn't have the heart to say, 'Move over.' "

> *Joe Altobelli, on Ronald Reagan sitting in Altobelli's seat in the dugout on Opening Day*

"These towns in the Pacific Coast League were getting a little old. A couple of them wanted me to run for mayor."

> *DeWayne Buice, on his long tenure in the minors*

"I'm not going to say too much about it. He might end up being our governor, and I don't want him to raise my taxes."

> *Scott Livingstone, a Texas native, on getting a hit off Nolan Ryan*

"If he can't run for office any better than he runs the Texas Rangers, he doesn't have any advantages."

> *Ed Martin, Texas Democratic party executive director, on Rangers owner George W. Bush's political ambitions*

"That's more than the Clinton administration is spending on arms."

> *Don McMillan, comedian, on the expense of signing the Braves pitching staff of Glavine, Smoltz, Maddux, and Avery*

"The Senators were never very good, but not much has changed in Washington. The senators they have there still aren't very good."

Richard Nixon

"I'm a Dominican."

Jose Rijo, on being asked if he were a Democrat or Republican

"Hotter 'n hell, ain't it, Prez?"

Babe Ruth, to President Calvin Coolidge

"What was I supposed to say? 'Glad you got over Watergate'?"

Steve Sax, after Richard Nixon told Sax he was glad he had gotten over his arm problems

"I stayed up late last night and watched the Republican convention all night long. I watched all of the talk and listened to them and saw them, and I'm not interested in politics. If you watch them and listen to them, you can find out why you're not."

Casey Stengel

"It was like Bush coming back to the Clinton inauguration."

> *Andy Van Slyke, on Barry Bonds coming back to Pittsburgh with the Giants for the first time*

POVERTY

"I was poor; my first contract was signed in dirt. . . . We spelled poor with only one *o*, because we ate the other one."

Mel Hall

"I'm so poor I can't even pay attention."

Ron Kittle

"The soles of my shoes were so thin, I could step on a coin and tell if it was heads or tails."

Tommy Lasorda

POWER

"We're not even going to catch Roger Maris."
> *Whitey Herzog, on a power-weak Cardinal's team*

"He has enough power to hit home runs in any park—including Yellowstone."
> *Paul Richards, on Harmon Killebrew*

PRACTICE

"You ever see a batting practice pitcher drop dead? Men drop dead shoveling snow but not pitching batting practice. That's why I pitch batting practice."
> *Tommy Lasorda*

"I got blisters from swinging eight billion times in practice, then I go 0 for 5 in the game."
> *Steve Lyons*

"The workout is optional. Whoever doesn't come gets optioned."

Bobby Valentine, on a tough workout

PRESSURE

"I took the baseball from Greg [Riddoch] and I said, 'Th-th-th-thanks.' "

Larry Andersen, on being called in with a one-run lead with the bases loaded and no outs in the ninth

"There's been pressure on me since I was born. My parents wanted a girl."

Lee Smith

PUNS

"That's a high chopper over the mound."

Dave Gallagher, on a helicopter over the mound at Tiger Stadium

"I heard you had a lot of power."

> *Ron Gant, on Vice President Gore taking some practice swings before a Braves game*

"I have just one goal—to be thumb-back player of the year."

> *Steve Garvey, on missing 62 games because of a thumb injury*

"Santiago flies to Chili."

> *Hank Greenwald, after Benito Santiago flew out to Chili Davis*

"The greased pig competition had to be canceled because the pig pulled a hamstring."

> *Richard Griffin, Expos PR director, on the cancellation of a pregame promotion featuring a pig*

"It looks like Cone burned the Candaele at both ends."

> *Tim McCarver, on David Cone striking out Casey Candaele on three pitches*

"Now he's one of the patients of Jobe."

> *Tim McCarver, on Pedro Guerrero undergoing surgery by Dr. Frank Jobe*

"You might say he's starting from scratch."

> *Vin Scully, on Alejandro Pena returning from a bout with the chicken pox*

"Does that make me a Hart specialist?"

> *Ron Swoboda, after pinch-running for Jim Ray Hart*

"Is that called 'dustin' ' Hoffman?"

> *Joe Torre, on a brushback pitch thrown at Glenn Hoffman*

QUOTES

"What's a Yogi-ism?"

> *Yogi Berra, after being told by Phil Garner that he had used a Yogi-ism*

"Nah. Somebody will think of something and designate it to a spokee to be named later."

> *Rocky Bridges, asked if he said everything he was supposed to have said*

"The game is not over until the sixth inning is over."

> *Lee Ming Chen, manager of a Little League team from Taiwan, translating a classic line*

"To err is human, to forgive divine. I forgot who said that, but I think it was Joey Amalfitano."

> *Tommy Lasorda*

RADIO

"Let's check out the replay on that one."

> *Johnny Pesky, doing radio play-by-play*

RECORDS

"I've never had a club record, except for car wrecks."
Darren Daulton, on setting the Phillies' record for most RBIs by a catcher

"You've got to lead the league in something."
Dale Mohorcic, on committing balks in his first two appearances of the season

REDS

"It's a good thing I stayed in Cincinnati for four years—it took me that long to learn how to spell it."
Rocky Bridges

"The Cincinnati Reds act like a drill team—they should be managed by Jack Webb."
Bill Lee, on the Big Red Machine

"We've definitely reached the highest level of embar-rassivity."

Jose Rijo, on a bad year for the Reds

"Throw a Visine ball. It gets the Red out."

Don Sutton, on former Reds star Eric Davis

REFEREES

═══════════════════════════════════════

"I get yelled at all summer, so I figure that I might as well get yelled at all winter too."

Scott Scudder, on being a basketball referee in the off-season

RELIEF PITCHING

═══════════════════════════════════════

"A lot of long relievers are ashamed to tell their parents what they do. The only nice thing about it is you get to wear a uniform like everybody else."

Jim Bouton

"A lot of things run through your head when you're going in to relieve in a tough spot. One of them was 'Should I spike myself?' "
Lefty Gomez

"Three more saves and he ties John the Baptist."
Hank Greenwald, on Bruce Sutter

"All of his saves have come during relief appearances."
Ralph Kiner, on Steve Bedrosian

"Why pitch nine innings when you can get just as famous pitching two?"
Sparky Lyle

"I enjoy being a reliever because I like getting 6 outs for the same money as getting 27."
Steve McCatty

"I don't throw hard enough to get a sore arm."
Dale Mohorcic, on appearing in 15 of 17 games

"A manager uses a relief pitcher like a six-shooter. He fires until it's empty and then takes the gun and throws it at the villain."

Dan Quisenberry

"We're parasites. We live off the people who spend two hours on the field."

Dan Quisenberry

"The bullpen is a nice place to visit, but I wouldn't want to live there."

Bill Singer

"Don't get used to it."

Mitch Williams, on pitching a one-two-three inning

RELIGION

"If God let you hit a home run last time up, then who struck you out the time before that?"

Sparky Anderson

"God is still my amigo, but he must be someplace else. Maybe he's watching the American League."

> *Joaquin Andujar, after leading the National League in losses*

"No, but I saw him."

> *Yogi Berra, asked if he had an audience with the pope*

"A Christian gets pennant fever just like everyone else."

> *Alvin Davis, on being a born-again Christian and being in a pennant race*

"We're 24 morons and a Mormon."

> *John Kruk, describing the Phillies when Dale Murphy was on the team*

"If it was that easy, Billy Graham would hit .400."

> *Chris Sabo, on Marge Schott suggesting that the Reds try praying to end a losing streak*

"After the kind of year we had, I've got to touch all the bases."

> *Bud Selig, Brewers owner, on meeting both the pope and the chief rabbi of Jerusalem after a bad season for the Brewers*

"I've always believed in God, but I wasn't too clear on the other details."

> *Bill Veeck*

"I'd rather you walk with the bases loaded."

> *Earl Weaver, after Pat Kelly told Weaver to "walk with the Lord"*

RESTAURANTS

"I look at baseball players as I do at restaurants—I love the expensive ones and despise the overpriced ones."

> *Danny Kaye*

"I don't care. They let me eat free."

Mickey Mantle, on a restaurant named after him

"The best way to avoid ballplayers is to go to a good restaurant."

Tim McCarver

RETIREMENT

"I'll make everybody more money that way. I know you guys have to have something to write about or you don't get paid. I'm just trying to help."

Joaquin Andujar, on deciding not to retire

"I'd become a professional go-getter. My wife would go to work, and I'd go get her."

Tim Flannery, on what he plans to do when he retires

"He wants to quit baseball and become a professional musician. The problem is he can't sing or play an instrument."

Carmen Franco, on her husband, Julio

"Us ballplayers do things backwards. First we play, then we retire and go to work."

Charlie Gehringer

"As I walked back to the dugout after striking out, I looked into the stands and saw my wife and kids booing me."

Fran Healy, on how he knew it was time to retire

"When your dentist's kid starts hitting you, it's time to go."

Tommy John, on Mark McGwire hitting him well

"I got tired of ducking line drives and backing up home plate."

Bob Miller, on deciding to retire

"In one day I went from a negative presence to a man with a great past."

Jim Palmer, on announcing his retirement

"It really bothers me to think I may never throw a home-run pitch again."

Jim Palmer, on his retirement

"The league will be a little drier now, folks."

Gaylord Perry, announcing his retirement

"Room service french fries."

Mike Schmidt, on what he misses most in retirement

"My arm has felt so bad since I retired that I can't even throw a tantrum."

Steve Stone

"They broke it to me gently. The manager came up to me before a game and told me they didn't allow visitors in the clubhouse."

Bob Uecker

"I married him for better or worse but not for lunch."

Mrs. George Weiss, after her husband retired as Yankees GM

ROAD TRIPS

"On this trip alone I've spent $1,200 on tips to bellmen to take luggage to my room."

Rich Donnelly, third-base coach, on a long Pirates road trip

"Take the fellows over to the other diamond—I want to see if they can play on the road."

Casey Stengel, during an intersquad practice

"It's like when your wife leaves her purse in a cab with $50 in cash and $10,000 in jewelry and she comes back with the jewelry."

Joe Torre, on a road trip that started with four losses in Atlanta and ended with three wins in Cincinnati

"On the road when you go downstairs for coffee in your underwear, they throw you out of the kitchen."

> *Andy Van Slyke, on the difference between road and home games*

ROOKIES

"Rick Sutcliffe was the rookie of the year in his first year."

> *Ralph Kiner*

ROYALTY

"Yeah, but they all talk to each other."

> *Brady Anderson, on being told that Queen Elizabeth, whom he and his Orioles teammates had just met, and Princess Caroline were not related*

RULES

"We live by the golden rule. Those who have the gold make the rules."

Buzzie Bavasi

"I try not to break the rules but merely to test their elasticity."

Bill Veeck

SAN DIEGO CHICKEN

"Why did you cross the road?"

Skip Caray, to the San Diego chicken

"Who knows? They've got a broadcaster's wing; they've got a player's wing. Maybe one day they'll have a chicken wing."

Ted Giannoulas, also known as the San Diego chicken, speculating on making the Hall of Fame

"We leave no wallaby untamed."

> *Sandy Alderson, on the A's sending a scout to Australia to check out a prospect*

"I once scouted a pitcher who was so bad that when he came into a game, the ground crew dragged the warning track."

> *Ellis Clary*

"My father looked at the check and then told the scout, 'Throw in another hundred and you can take the rest of the family.' "

> *Joe Dugan, on signing for a $500 bonus in the early 1920s*

SEX

"I'd rather hit than have sex."

> *Reggie Jackson*

"You gotta learn that if you don't get it by midnight, chances are you ain't gonna get it; if you do, it ain't worth it."

Casey Stengel

"Going to bed with a woman the night before a game never hurt a ballplayer. It's staying up all night looking for one that does him in."

Casey Stengel

SHOWERS

"By the time the hot water reaches you, it's cold."

Lefty Gomez, on the high ceilings in the showers at Sportsman's Park

"Once I tried to drown myself with a shower nozzle after I gave up a home run in the ninth. I found out you can't."

Dan Quisenberry

SIGNS

"Don't worry about that. I'll give each of you the ones you use on your team."

> *Charlie Dressen, master sign stealer,*
> *when asked during the All-Star Game*
> *what signs the National League team*
> *should use*

"If they were any simpler, I'd be using flash cards."

> *Dick Williams*

SINGLES HITTERS

"You can't change to a .22 when you've gone with a .44 magnum for 19 years."

> *Reggie Jackson, on why he refused to*
> *end his career as a singles hitter*

"If I had as many singles as Pete Rose, I'd have worn a dress."

> *Mickey Mantle*

SKYDOME

"Ever hear the saying 'there's a fly in my soup?' Well, there was a fly ball in that guy's soup."

> Dave Henderson, on Cecil Fielder's home run into the center-field restaurant in the SkyDome

SLIDES

"They're safer and faster. And they usually get your picture in the paper."

> Pete Rose, on why he prefers headfirst slides

"He couldn't cut me if he hit me in the lip with a fastball."

> *Roger Craig, on Bob Ojeda*

"I think he threw harder than me."

> *Charlie Hough, on Joe DiMaggio throwing out the first ball at the Marlins' inaugural game*

"You could almost walk alongside them."

> *Lon Simmons, announcer, on Tommy John's slow pitches*

"In the '70s I threw in the 90s. In the '90s, I throw in the 70s."

> *Frank Tanana*

"He really tantalized them. I never saw him so slow."

> *El Tappe, on slow-ball pitcher Jack Curtis winning a game*

"You can time his stuff with a squirt gun."

> *Dave Winfield, on DeWayne Buice*

"They should trade me for a Class A pitcher, a 50th-round draft choice, and a bucket of balls."

Shawn Abner, after a miserable slump

"Slump? I ain't in no slump. I just ain't hitting."

Yogi Berra

"I'm the only man in the history of the game who began his career in a slump and stayed in it."

Rocky Bridges

"If I get a hit, I might stop the game and ask for the ball."

Tom Brunansky, during an 0–34 slump

"I'm in a slump. I go to bed and I'm hungry. I sit down at the table and I get romantic."

Tommy Lasorda

"We gotta trade him when he's still hot."

> *Casey Stengel, on Don Zimmer getting two hits in a row after being in an 0–34 slump*

"We're in such a slump that even the ones that are drinking aren't hitting."

> *Casey Stengel*

"Maybe you can talk the other team into throwing to you underhanded."

> *A. J. Van Slyke, seven-year-old son of Andy Van Slyke, during a batting slump*

"I have an Alka-Seltzer bat. You know plop, plop, fizz, fizz. When the pitcher sees me walking up there, they say, 'Oh, what a relief it is.' "

> *Andy Van Slyke*

"I thought they would have given this to me in May when I was batting about .088."

> *Ozzie Virgil, on taking a drug test*

"I've been doing my best not to think about it, but by trying so hard not to think about it I can't stop thinking about it."

Paul Zuvella, on a slump

SMALL TOWNS

"I live so far out in the country that I have to walk towards town to go hunting."

Rocky Bridges

"The telephone directory has only one yellow page."

Toby Harrah, on his hometown

SPEED

"Coaching third with a pitcher on base is like being a member of a bomb-disposal squad. The thing can blow up in your face at any minute."

Rocky Bridges

"There was nothing to lose."

Ron Fairly, asked if he had lost any speed at the age of 40

"The wind always seems to be blowing against catchers when they are running."

Joe Garagiola

"Bruce Benedict is so slow, he'd finish third in a race with a pregnant woman."

Tommy Lasorda

"One time he hit a line drive right past my ear. I turned around and saw the ball hit his ass sliding into second base."

Satchel Paige, on Cool Papa Bell

"Let's put it this way—pigeons have been roosting on him for two years."

Vin Scully, on Ron Cey's mobility around third base

"His only limitation is his ability to move around."

Joe Torre, on Pedro Guerrero

"Rich Dauer is so slow that we time him from home to first with a calendar."

Earl Weaver

SPITBALLS

"Not intentionally, but I sweat easily."

Lefty Gomez, asked if he threw spitters

"He talks very well for a guy with two fingers in his mouth all the time."

Gene Mauch, on Don Drysdale

"I played golf with him, and he wouldn't admit to my friend that he threw a spitter. I said, 'Heck, Lew, I used to call it for you.'"

Tim McCarver, on Lew Burdette

"When Lew was a 20-game winner for the Milwaukee Braves, papers needed three columns for his pitching record: won, lost, and relative humidity."

Red Smith, on Lew Burdette

"I'd like to write my own column, but I'd have too many spelling mistakes."

> *Barry Bonds, on plans to write his own sports column*

"The Lord taught me to love everybody, but the last ones I learned to love were the sportswriters."
> *Alvin Dark*

"I'll have to gain 60 pounds, start smoking a cigar, and wear clothes that don't match."

> *Garth Iorg, on plans to write a sports column for the* Toronto Star

"I always thought that to win a Pulitzer you have to bring down a government, not just quote Tommy Lasorda correctly."

> *Jim Murray, on winning a Pulitzer Prize*

"I know when to get a guy in the bottom of the ninth, with two outs, the bases loaded, and us down by three runs, to come up to the plate as a pinch hitter and hit a home run. I just can't get him away from his typewriter in the press box."

> *Danny Murtaugh, on the second-guessers in the press box*

"I like my horses better because they can't talk to sportswriters."

> *George Steinbrenner, on why he likes his horses better than his players*

"To hell with sportswriters. You can buy any of them with a steak."

> *George Weiss*

SPRING TRAINING

"When I was young, I would have worried about it. But those days are long gone."

> *Sparky Anderson, on the Tigers committing a lot of errors during spring training*

"Florida is for old people and their parents."

Harry Dalton, on why he favors Arizona as a spring training site

"The last time I was in shorts, I was fired."

Billy Gardner, on why he doesn't wear shorts during spring training

"In a couple of weeks all the averages will go back to zero. Howard just won't have as far to go."

Davey Johnson, on Howard Johnson hitting .115 in spring training

"Spring training should last one day. We'd have the team golf outing and head north."

John Kruk

"Spring is a time of year when the ground thaws, trees bud, the income tax falls due, and everybody wins the pennant."

Jim Murray

"I could wind up at second, I could wind up at third, or I could wind up working the snack bar."

Steve Sax, on being unsure of his status during spring training

"That's the true harbinger of spring—not crocuses or swallows returning to Capistrano but the sound of a bat on a ball."

Bill Veeck

STATISTICS

"Statistics are about as interesting as first-base coaches."

Jim Bouton

"Statistics are to baseball what a flaky crust is to Mom's apple pie."

Harry Reasoner

"Statistics are used like a drunk uses a lamppost—for support, not illumination."

Vin Scully

"It was a beautiful thing to behold, with all 30 oars working in unison."

> *Jack Buck, on George Steinbrenner's yacht*

"Nothing is more limited than being a limited partner of George's."

> *Jim McMullen, on owning a small part of the Yankees*

"George is always trying to patch up the tire when the car needs a new set of wheels."

> *Lou Piniella*

"My friend Bo [the Annapolis athletic director] asked me if I believed in free speech. I said I certainly did. He said, 'Fine, you're giving one at the Naval Academy.'"

> *George Steinbrenner*

STENGELESE

"It was the first role I ever played in a foreign language."

Charles Durning, on performing a one-man show on Casey Stengel

STOLEN BASES

"There was larceny in his heart, but his feet were honest."

Bugs Baer, on the slow-footed Ping Bodie trying to steal a base

"I couldn't resist. I had such a great jump on the pitch."

Lou Novikoff, on trying to steal third with the bases loaded

"The only way you can do that is by breaking into the equipment room."

> *Pete Rose, on Greg Luzinski's claims that he would steal 20 bases*

"Some guys just always get the green light."

> *Nolan Ryan, on being thrown out trying to steal a base*

"When he runs, it's always downhill."

> *Vin Scully, on Maury Wills*

"Can't make a racehorse out of a mule."

> *Harry Spilman, on going more than seven years without a stolen base*

STRENGTH

"He is strong enough to throw a soft-boiled egg through a battleship."

> *Blackie Sherrod, sportswriter, on Don Drysdale*

"A woman will be elected president before Wade Boggs is called out on strikes."

>*George Brett*

"Prorated at 500 at-bats a year, that means that for two years out of the 14 I played, I never touched the ball."

>*Norm Cash, on his 1,081 career strikeouts*

"Well, I guess I was just in the right place at the right time."

>*Outfielder Cesar Geronimo, on being the 3,000th strikeout victim for both Bob Gibson and Nolan Ryan*

"When I played, it was the shoulders to the knees. Now it's the top of the belt buckle to the bottom."

>*Lefty Gomez, on the shrinking strike zone*

"I'm a slow starter."

> *Billy Grabarkewitz, on having fewer strikeouts early in '73 than early in previous seasons*

"Charley showed us he could hit three ways—left, right, and seldom."

> *Joe Klein, former Rangers GM, on Charlie Pride, country singer and former minor league ballplayer, striking out in an exhibition game*

"Nick took two third strikes—proving he is in mid-season form."

> *Al Lopez, on Dave Nicholson striking out a lot in spring training*

"He passed me on the all-time strikeout list a couple of years ago, and nobody asked me about that."

> *Mickey Mantle, on Reggie Jackson passing him on the all-time home-run list*

"[Willie Mays] was something like 0 for 21 the first time I faced him. His first major league hit was a home run off me, and I'll never forgive myself. We might have gotten rid of Willie forever if only I'd struck him out."

Warren Spahn

SUCCESS

"I've learned how to handle the adversity of success."
Fred Toliver

SUPERSTITIONS

"None, really. I never pitch well on days they play the national anthem."

Mike Flanagan, asked if he had any superstitions

"I had only one superstition. I made sure to touch all four bases when I hit a home run."
Babe Ruth

SWITCH HITTERS

"He's a better interview from the left side than the right side."

Al Michaels, joking about an interview with switch hitter Bobby Bonilla

TELEVISION

"If the World Series runs seven games, it will be our longest-running show this fall."

Johnny Carson, on a bad year for NBC

"That will come on 'Wide World of Sports' right after the guy who falls off the ski slope."

Alan Knicely, on a popup that hit him on the head

"Doing TV backup games is like holding a telethon for hiccups."

Ron Luciano

"What would I do that for? It only gets Spanish stations."

> *Jeff Stone, asked why he wouldn't bring his TV back to the United States after playing winter ball in Venezuela*

THINKING

"How can a guy think and hit at the same time."
> *Yogi Berra*

"I think too much on the mound sometimes, and I get brain cramps."
> *Britt Burns*

"I never tried to outsmart nobody; it was easier to outdummy them."
> *Dizzy Dean*

"If you think long, you think wrong."
> *Jim Kaat*

"When you start thinkin' is when you get your ass beat."

Sparky Lyle

THREE RIVERS STADIUM

"My father's cemetery has more life in it than this ballpark."

Richie Hebner

TIME-OUTS

"Please tell me you were trying to stop the clock because we were out of time-outs."

Jim Leyland, on Jay Bell throwing balls into the stands at Three Rivers Stadium

TRADES

"I'd carry Steve Jeltz on my back all the way to K.C. and drop him off at home plate to make that trade."

Hugh Alexander, Cubs scout, on Steve Jeltz being traded for Jose DeJesus, who throws a 95 mph fastball

"I'll have to go out and get another life insurance policy. I'm worth more than I thought."

Joey Amalfitano, on being traded for $125,000 in the early '60s

"We played him, and now we can't trade him."

Buzzie Bavasi, on Don Zimmer's play-me-or-trade-me ultimatum

"I've had more numbers on my back than a bingo board."

Rocky Bridges

"My wife had to write me care of Ford Frick."

Rocky Bridges, on being on 7 different teams in 11 years

"I was the glue that held the Red Sox together."

Jack Brohamer, after the Red Sox lost
26–2 on the day after he was traded

"Being traded is like celebrating your 100th birthday. It might not be the happiest occasion in the world, but consider the alternative."

Joe Garagiola

"A very even trade."

Rich Griffin, on Archie Corbin being
traded from Montreal to Milwaukee
for a player to be named later—who
turned out to be Corbin

"I'm never one to bear a grudge. If I did, I'd hate half the teams in the American League."

Paul Mirabella, on being picked back
up by Seattle after being cut by the
Mariners and several other teams over
the years

"From Cy Young to sayonara in one year."

Graig Nettles, on Sparky Lyle going
from being the Cy Young Award win-
ner to being traded by the Yankees

"I'm not sure which is more insulting, being offered in a trade or having it turned down."

Claude Osteen

"My flowers just came up, my shrubbery looks good, my grass is really seeded well. To leave all that would be devastating."

Andy Van Slyke, on trade rumors involving him

TRIPLE PLAYS

"Joe Morgan told us we had to stay out of double plays, and we did."

Dennis Lamp, after the Red Sox hit into two triple plays in a game

UGLY

"This guy's wife was so ugly, he took her on road trips because he couldn't stand to kiss her good-bye."

Rocky Bridges

"He's so ugly that when a fly ball was hit towards him, it would curve away from him."

Mickey Rivers, on Danny Napoleon

UMPIRES

"How could he be doing his job when he didn't throw me out of the game after the things I called him?"

Mark Belanger, on arguing with ump Russ Goetz

"I occasionally get birthday cards from fans. But it's often the same message: they hope it's my last one."

Al Foreman, former major league umpire

"An umpire is like a woman. He makes quick decisions, never reverses them, and doesn't think you're safe when you're out."

Larry Goetz

"It's a strange business—all jeers and no cheers."

Tom Gorman, on umpiring

"When I am right, no one remembers. When I am wrong, no one forgets."

Doug Harvey

"Well, then I think you are doing a lousy job."

Cleon Jones, when he asked an umpire if he could get thrown out for thinking and the umpire said no

"I called a lot of baa-rikes and stri-alls."

Ron Luciano, on often being confused behind the plate

"A bad call in baseball is one that goes against you."

Danny Murtaugh

"Plenty of players will like that."

Joe West, umpire, on playing a guy in a movie who gets shot

"Because they wouldn't give me my favorite number: no. 5081782."

> *Gates Brown, former convict, on why he wears number 26*

"There's someone warming up in the bullpen, but he's obscured by his number."

> *Jerry Coleman*

"Is that your age or the number of teams you've been with?"

> *Eddie Fisher, on Dick Schofield wearing the number 58*

"All the women will say, 'There goes Tom Kelly. He's a 10.'"

> *Tom Kelly, on changing from number 41 to number 10*

"That touched me. In Atlanta, Ozzie Virgil offered to *sell* me his number."

> *Graig Nettles, when new teammate*
> *Casey Candaele offered to give Nettles*
> *his old Yankees number after a trade*

"I want to make sure nobody's in my uniform."

> *Don Zimmer, on why he arrives early*
> *for games*

UTILITY PLAYERS

"I'm an eclipse player. You don't see me very often."

> *Benny Ayala*

"I think I hold the record for most games watched, career."

> *Kurt Bevacqua*

"I experienced a fantasy of my own. I got to play an entire game."

> *Kurt Bevacqua, former utility player,*
> *on playing an entire fantasy league*
> *game*

"They ought to change our name to the Cleveland Light Company. We don't have anything but utility men."

>*Lou Camilli, on the Indians of the early '60s*

"So far I've played right, left, and first base, and I'm Polish. Does that make me a utility Pole?"

>*Frank Kostro*

"Play me or keep me."

>*Phil Linz*

VETERANS STADIUM

"There's so much tobacco juice all over the rug, you can get cancer by just standing out there. It's like a toxic waste dump."

>*Andy Van Slyke, on center field at Veterans Stadium, Len Dykstra's home field*

"Thanks. You don't look so hot yourself."
> *Yogi Berra, after being told he looked cool in his summer suit*

"It was like we were playing drunk out there."
> *Ellis Burks, on a windy day in Oakland*

"It was so cold that ice was forming in my spitter."
> *Dick Farrell, on 30-degree temperatures during a game*

"I don't think I should be asked to catch when the temperature is below my age."
> *Carlton Fisk, on a frigid day at age 43*

"It's so cold, the ice feels warm compared to the air."
> *Bill Lee, on living in Vermont*

"We got to freeze our butts and get them kicked at the same time."

Lou Piniella, on the Mariners losing 20–3 on a 38-degree day

"I give your five-day roll-on about two hours."
Vin Scully, on Miami weather

"I don't think it will affect his mobility. Electrical storms might be a problem."

Jeff Torborg, on a metal plate inserted in Carlton Fisk's right arm

WEIGHT

"Like they say, it ain't over till the fat guy swings."
Darren Daulton, on John Kruk

"Let's not overdo this. I only have to call the bases, not steal them."

Eric Gregg, 300-pound umpire, on having to lose weight

"I can't help how I look, but I hate it when guys on the other team yell at me, 'Hey, get that hamburger out of your back pocket.'"

Tony Gwynn

"If it had been a cheeseburger, he would have caught it."

Keith Hernandez, after the overweight Dave LaPoint missed an easy toss from Keith Hernandez during the '82 World Series

"I have a wife who reads eat-to-win books. Is it my fault if I take my wife seriously?"

Dave LaPoint

"I have to watch my playing weight. But the problem is that I don't know what my playing weight is. I never play."

Joe Lis

"We're given a choice. We can either run around the field three times or run around Tommy Lasorda once."

Steve Sax, on the formerly overweight Lasorda

"You know what you're going to have with all those weight clauses—25 Manute Bols."

>*Rick Sutcliffe, on teams that have required players to come in below a specified weight*

"I don't need a chest protector. I need a bra."

>*Gus Triandos, on being an overweight catcher during an Old-Timers Game*

WHITE SOX

"Our 1976 White Sox team was so bad that by the fifth inning Bill Veeck was selling hot dogs to go."

>*Ken Brett*

"I have found that every five years a man has to change his Sox."

>*Infielder Steve Lyons, when he signed with the Red Sox in 1991 after five years with the White Sox*

"Grantland Rice, the great sportswriter, once said, 'It's not whether you win or lose, it's how you play the game.' Well, Grantland Rice can go to hell as far as I'm concerned."

Gene Autry

"The other teams could make trouble for us if they win."

Yogi Berra, on the Yankees' chances in 1964

"Win any way you can as long as you can get away with it."

Leo Durocher

"Winning isn't as important as doing well individually. You can't take teamwork up to the front office to negotiate."

Ken Landreaux

"It's like walking down the street with a bulldog. We have no fear."

> *Tommy Lasorda, after the Dodgers won five of their first six games*

"If you don't play to win, why keep score?"
> *Vern Law*

"That was a maximization of a minimization of hits."
> *Mike Macfarlane, after Kansas City won a game 3–1 with only one hit*

"Root only for the winner. That way you won't be disappointed."
> *Tug McGraw*

"When we lost, I couldn't sleep at night. When we win, I can't sleep at night. But when you win, you wake up feeling better."
> *Joe Torre*

"I'm not emotionally suited for any occupation in which you can be hailed as a success if you lose 'only' 62 times in a year."
> *Edward Bennett Williams*

WINNING STREAKS

"If they had just traded me the day before the season started, they'd be 120–0."

> *Roger McDowell, on the Phillies winning 12 games in a row after trading him*

"It's a shame to have a day off when we're hot."

> *Tom Trebelhorn, on winning a game after losing 12 in a row and then having an off-day*

WOMEN

"The more French women I meet, the more French I learn."

> *Hubie Brooks, on playing in Montreal*

"Mitch found God in spring training. Then every night he went looking for a goddess."

> *Len Dykstra, on Kevin Mitchell*

"In the daytime you sat in the dugout and talked about women. At night you went out with women and talked about baseball."

Waite Hoyt, on baseball in the old days

WORK

"Dave, I wanted to be like you: I didn't want to work."

Reggie Jackson, explaining to David Letterman why he wanted to play baseball

"Putting on a uniform, jumping around in the dirt, and getting paid for it just ain't work."

Rick Jones, Mariners prospect

"I'm a vice president in charge of special marketing. That means I play golf and go to cocktail parties. I'm pretty good at my job."

Mickey Mantle

"I'm proud of my sons and happy they don't have to work for a living."

> *Phil Niekro, Sr., on his sons, Phil and Joe*

WORLD SERIES

"When we played, World Series checks meant something. Now all they do is screw up your taxes."
> *Don Drysdale*

"Clean living and a fast outfield."
> *Lefty Gomez, explaining his great World Series record*

WRIGLEY FIELD

"If we went by tradition, we'd still be playing without gloves."

> *Jim Frey, asked his opinion on lights at Wrigley Field*

"Instead of going to nightclubs, you go to happy hour."

> *Gary Matthews, on playing at Wrigley Field when it had only day games*

"I favor blowing this place up."

> *Keith Moreland, when asked if he favored night games at Wrigley Field*

"Putting lights in Wrigley Field is like putting aluminum siding on the Sistine Chapel."

> *Roger Simon, columnist*

"They're the same—no parking around either one."

> *Lee Smith, on comparing Wrigley Field to Fenway Park*

YANKEES

"There are close to 11 million unemployed, and half of them are New York Yankees managers."

> *Johnny Carson*

"Why would George Steinbrenner want me? Did he fire his limo driver?"

> *Mickey Hatcher, on rumors that the Yankees were interested in acquiring him*

"Shut up, you guys, or I'll put on a Yankees uniform and scare the shit out of all of you."

> *Waite Hoyt, on being hassled by opponents late in his career while playing for the Pirates*

"The Yankees are America's team. You know—Mom, apple pie, Gucci loafers, Rolls-Royces."

> *Tommy John*

"When I was a kid, I wanted to play baseball and join the circus. With the Yankees, I've been able to do both."

> *Graig Nettles*

"The reason the Yankees never lay an egg is because they don't operate on chicken feed."

> *Dan Parker*

"The two biggest expenses for Yankee employees—
coming and going-away parties."
Bob Quinn

YANKEES FANS

"Seeing Yankees fans up close for the first time is like
waking up in a Brazilian jail."
Art Hill

YANKEE STADIUM

"It gets late early out there."
*Yogi Berra, on the shadows in Yankee
Stadium*

"Pearson, Ruth, DiMaggio, Barrow, Rupert, throw the ball in."

Rocky Bridges, after Albie Pearson retrieved a ball hit to the monuments at Yankee Stadium

"There's no way they can bury 12 people out there."

Bob Kearney, on the 12 monuments in Yankee Stadium

INDEX

*An asterisk appears before names that are referred to in a quote. All other names are the actual sources of a quote.

228